KABBALAH CENTRE BOOKS

The Zohar 24 volumes by Rabbi Shimon bar Yoḥai, *The cardinal work in the literature of Kabbalah. Original Aramaic text with Hebrew translation and commentary by Rabbi Yehudah Ashlag*

Miracles, Mysteries, and Prayer Volume I, Rabbi Berg (also available in Spanish and Russian)

Kabbalah for the Layman Volume I, Rabbi Berg (also available in Hebrew, Spanish, French, Russian, Italian, German, Persian, Chinese and Portuguese)

Kabbalah for the Layman Volumes II, III, Rabbi Berg (also available in Hebrew, Spanish, French and Italian)

Wheels of a Soul Rabbi Berg (also available in Hebrew, Spanish, French, Russian, Italian, and Persian)

Astrology: The Star Connection, The Science of Judaic Astrology Rabbi Berg (also available in Hebrew, Spanish, French and Persian)

Time Zones: Creating Order from Chaos Rabbi Berg (also available in French, Spanish, Hebrew and Persian)

To The Power of One Rabbi Berg (also available in French and Spanish)

Power of the Aleph Beth Volumes I, II, Rabbi Berg (also available in Hebrew, French and Spanish)

The Kabbalah Connection Rabbi Berg (also available in Spanish and Hebrew)

Kabbalistik Astrology Made Easy Rabbi Berg in French Translation

Gift of the Bible Rabbi Yehudah Ashlag, Foreword by Rabbi Berg (also available in French, Hebrew and Spanish)

Zohar: Parashat Pinḥas Volumes I, II, III, Translated , compiled and edited by Rabbi Berg (also available in Spanish)

An Entrance to the Tree of Life Rabbi Yehudah Ashlag, Compiled and edited by Rabbi Berg (also available in Spanish)

Ten Luminous Emanations Rabbi Yehudah Ashlag, Volumes I, II, Compiled and edited by Rabbi Berg (also available in Hebrew , 7 Volume set)

An Entrance to The Zohar Rabbi Yehudah Ashlag, Compiled and edited by Rabbi Berg

General Principles of Kabbalah Rabbi M. Luzzatto (also available in Italian)

Light of Redemption by Rabbi Levi Krakovsky

Kabbalistik Children's Stories:

Heaven on Your Head, Tales of the Enlightened, Legends of Israel, Legends of Zion DR. S. Z. Kahana

SOON TO BE PUBLISHED

Secret Codes of the Universe Rabbi Berg

Kabbalistik Astrology Made Easy Rabbi Berg

Ten Luminous Emanations Volumes III, IV, Rabbi Yehudah Ashlag , compiled and edited by Rabbi Berg

Miracles, Mysteries, and Prayer Volume I, II, Rabbi Berg, in French Translation

Time Zones: Creating Order from Chaos Rabbi Berg, in Russian Translation

To The Power of One Rabbi Berg, in Russian Translation

Gift of the Bible Rabbi Yehudah Ashlag, Foreword by Rabbi Berg, in Russian Translation

BOOKS AND TAPES AVAILABLE
AT BOOKSELLERS AND KABBALAH CENTRES AROUND THE WORLD

MIRACLES, MYSTERIES, AND PRAYER

VOLUME TWO

KABBALAH

MIRACLES, MYSTERIES, AND PRAYER

VOLUME TWO

RABBI BERG

FIRST PRINTING
April 1993
SECOND PRINTING
July 1995

0-924457-90-2 (Soft Cover)

For further information:

THE KABBALAH LEARNING CENTRE
83-84 115th Street, Richmond Hill
NEW YORK, 11418
Tel. (718) 805-9122

— or —

P.O. BOX 14168
THE OLD CITY, JERUSALEM

PRINTED IN U.S.A.
1995

For a stronger spiritual connection with
the light, for a real inner change,
to bring more sharing
and love for no reason,
for the correct sequence in life
that will bring the fulfillment
of all wishes and the fulfillment of the
spiritual vessel,
to help bring the coming of Mashiach to
all of Israel and the whole world,

Braucha Bat Moshe Mordehi

For my wife,
Karen,
In the vastness of cosmic space
and infinity of lifetimes,
it is my bliss
to share with you,
my soulmate,
the Age of Aquarius.

ABOUT THE CENTRES

Kabbalah is mystical Judaism. It is the deepest and most hidden meaning of the Torah, or Bible. Through the ultimate knowledge and mystical practices of Kabbalah one can reach the highest spiritual levels attainable. Many people rely on belief, faith and dogma in pursuing the meaning of life, the unknown and the unseen. Yet, Kabbalists seek a spiritual connection with the Creator and the forces of the Creator. The strange thus becomes familiar, and faith becomes knowledge.

Throughout history, those who knew and practiced the Kabbalah were extremely careful in their dissemination of the knowledge — for they knew the masses of mankind had not yet been prepared for the ultimate truth of existence. Today Kabbalists know that it is not only proper, but necessary, to make the Kabbalah available to all who seek it.

The Kabbalah Learning Centre is an independent, non-profit institute founded in Israel in 1922. The Centre provides research, information and assistance to those who seek the insights of Kabbalah. The Centre offers public lectures, classes, seminars and excursions to mystical sites at branches in Israel — in Jerusalem, Tel Aviv, Haifa, Beer Sheva — and in the United States in New York and Los Angeles. Branches have been opened in Mexico, Toronto, Florida, North Miami, Paris, and London. Thousands of people have benefited by the Centre's activities. The publication of its Kabbalistic material continues to be the most comprehensive of its kind in the world. It includes translations in English, Hebrew, Russian, German, Portuguese, French, Spanish, Farsi (Persian) and Chinese.

Kabbalah can provide true meaning in one's being and the knowledge necessary for one's ultimate benefit. It can point towards a spirituality beyond belief. The Research Centre of Kabbalah will continue to make the Kabbalah available to all those who seek it.

ABOUT THE ZOHAR

The ZOHAR, the basic source of the Kabbalah was written by Rabbi Shimon bar Yohai while in hiding from the Romans in a cave in Pe'quin for 13 years. It was later brought to light by Rabbi Moses de Leon in Spain, and further revealed through the Safed Kabbalists and the Lurianic system of Kabbalah.

The programs of the Research Centre of Kabbalah have been established to provide opportunities for learning, teaching, research and demonstration of specialized knowledge drawn from the ageless wisdom of the Zohar and the Jewish Sages. Long kept from the masses, today this knowledge should be shared by all who seek to understand the deeper meaning of our Jewish heritage, a more profound meaning of life. Modern science is only beginning to discover what our Sages veiled in symbolism. This knowledge is of a very practical nature and can be applied daily for the betterment of our lives and of humankind.

Our courses and materials deal with the Zoharic understanding of each weekly portion of the Torah. Every facet of Jewish life is covered and other dimensions, hitherto unknown, provide a deeper connection to a superior Reality. Three important introductory courses cover such aspects as: Time, Space and Motion; Reincarnation, Marriage, Divorce, Kabbalistic Meditation, Limitation of the five senses, Illusion-Reality, Four Phases, Male and Female, Death, Sleep, Dreams; Food: what is kosher and why; Circumcision, Redemption of the First Born, *Shatnes, Shabbat.*

Darkness cannot prevail in the presence of Light. A darkened room must respond even to the lighting of a candle. As we share this moment together we are beginning to witness a people's revolution of enlightenment. And indeed, some of us are already participating in it. The darkened clouds of strife and conflict will make their presence felt only as long as the Eternal Light remains concealed.

The Zohar now remains a final, if not the only, solution to infusing the cosmos with the revealed Light of the Force. The Zohar is not a book about religion. Rather, the Zohar is concerned with the relationship between the unseen forces of the cosmos, the Force and Its impact on Man.

The Zohar promises that, with the ushering in of the Age of Aquarius, the cosmos will become readily accessible to human understanding. It states, that in the days of the Messiah, "there will no longer be the necessity for one to request of his neighbor, teach me wisdom" (Zohar III, p.58a). "One day they will no longer teach every man his neighbor and every man his brother, saying know the Lord. For they shall all know Me, from the youngest to the oldest of them" (Jeremiah 31:34).

We can and must regain control of our lives and environment. To achieve this objective the Zohar provides us with an opportunity to transcend the crushing weight of universal negativity.

The daily perusing of the Zohar, without any attempt at translation or "understanding" will fill our consciousness with the Light, improving our well-being and influencing everything in our environment toward positive attitudes. Even the scanning of the Zohar by those unfamiliar with the Hebrew Aleph Beth will accomplish the same result.

The connection that we establish through scanning the Zohar is a connection and unity with the Light of the Lord. The letters, even if we do not consciously know Hebrew or Aramaic, are the channels through which the connection is made. They could be likened to the dialing of the right telephone number, or the typing in the right codes to run a computer program. The connection is established at the metaphysical level of our being and radiates into our physical plane of existence...but first the metaphysical "mending" must take place. Through positive thoughts and actions we have to consciously permit the immense power of the Zohar to radiate love, harmony and peace into our lives — for us to share with all of humanity and the universe.

As we enter the years ahead, the Zohar will continue to be a people's book, striking a sympathetic chord in the hearts and minds of those who long for peace, truth and relief from suffering. In the face of crises and catastrophe it has the ability to resolve agonizing human afflictions by restoring each individual's relationship with the Force.

ABOUT THE AUTHOR

RABBI BERG is Dean of the Research Centre of Kabbalah. Born in New York City, into a family descended from a long line of Rabbis, he is an ordained Orthodox Rabbi (from the renowned rabbinical seminary Torat VaDaat). While traveling to Israel in 1962, he met his teacher, the distinguished Kabbalist Rabbi Yehudah Zvi Brandwein, student of Rabbi Yehudah Ashlag Z"L and then Dean of the Research Centre of Kabbalah. During that period the Centre expanded substantially with the establishment of the United States branch in 1965 through which it currently disseminates and distributes its publications. Rabbi Berg did research at the Centre under the auspices of his beloved teacher Rabbi Brandwein Z"L, writing books on such topics as the origins of Kabbalah, creation, cosmic consciousness, energy, and the myths of the speed of light and the light barrier. Following the death of his master in 1969, Rabbi Berg assumed the position of Dean of the Centre. He expanded its publication program through the translation of source material on the Kabbalah into English and other languages. Rabbi Berg moved with his devoted and dedicated wife Karen to Israel in 1971, where they opened the doors of the Centre to all seekers of self identity. They established centres in all major cities throughout Israel, while at the same time lecturing at the City University of Tel Aviv. They returned to the United States in 1981 to further found centres of learning in major cities all over the world. In addition to publishing scientific and popular articles, Rabbi Berg is the author, translator and/or editor of eighteen other books, including the *Kabbalah for the Layman* series, *Wheels of a Soul*, and *Time Zones*.

ACKNOWLEDGEMENTS

I would like to express my gratitude to Roy Tarlow for compiling, reviewing and editing the manuscript. He made fundamental and frequent contributions to the essential ideas and their connections to the overall style. The delight I found in our many discussions is one of my principal rewards from this book. Many heartfelt thanks to him for his helpful suggestions and careful proofreading of the manuscript.

TABLE OF CONTENTS

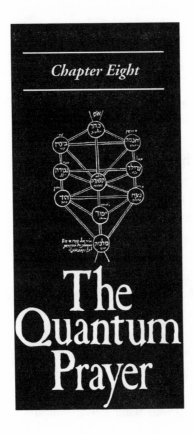

Chapter Eight

The Quantum Prayer

THE TASK OF STRIPPING AWAY OUR ROBOTIC-CONSCIOUSNESS is by no means an easy one. Nevertheless, states the Zohar, this is the *only* available approach to the enhancement of our physical and mental well-being. We must adjust and direct our consciousness to the realities of the "paradox." Otherwise, we follow the path of all flesh.

A similar idea of the paradoxical nature in the art of connection and linkage to contentment and order is presented in another section of the Zohar.[148]

> Rabbi Yosi discoursed on the verse:[149] "A prayer of the poor when he feels faint [or wrapped around] and pours out his complaint before the Lord." He said: As has been established in many

places, this psalm was composed by King David when he contemplated the plight of the poor man, and that was when he fled from his father-in-law. It was then that he composed a "prayer of the poor" as much as to say: Behold, this is the prayer a poor man offers up to the Lord, one which should ascend in advance of all other prayers.

Upon first glance, one might conclude that the Lord gives preference to the prayers of the "poor." Inasmuch as their plight and needs appear to be out of desperation, it only follows that the Lord listens first to the less fortunate. However, on second thought how does one determine who or what is considered poor. Reflect upon a marriage or any other relationship that has gone sour or wound up as a "poor" relationship. Someone in "poor" health, would not, in the words of King David, be answered "in advance of all other prayers."

Looking a bit closer at the Zoharic text the Zohar states that "this psalm was composed by King David when he contemplated the plight of the poor man, and that was when he fled from his father-in-law, King Saul."[150] Within the context stated we might assume that one running for his life is the definition of a poor man, to the possible exclusion of other troubles of a poor man such as finances, relationships or health.

Why would running for one's life designate this individual's prayer as one to be answered in advance of all other prayers? Serious prayer begins when the illusion that we are masters of our own fate fades and we develop an urgent need to call on the Master of the Universe. King David was fleeing from his predecessor and father-in-law, King Saul, who was bent on eliminating King David as a serious contender to the throne of Israel.

During this period, David had no illusions as to what sort of assistance and support he needed. He was, at this time, convinced that marital relationship, economic security or a desire for good health were of no importance to him. He no longer felt the need to master these necessities. They were of no concern to him; the desire to stay alive was his concern. He experienced the sensation of things existing beyond his control. David was indeed poor from the standpoint of consciousness of dominion over his affairs.

Consequently, he underwent a quantum-like sensation of a desire to receive. Thus, he appealed to the quantum "Desire to Share" of the Lightforce, without any reservations or uncertainties concerning his needs, creating the maximum affinity with the quantum feature of the Lightforce, which is the infinite "Desire to Share" Its beneficence with a "Desire to Receive" without limit. Thus, two opposing forces bring about a unity of opposites, a paradox similar to the Kabbalistic doctrine where one receives to the extent that one resists that which is deemed necessary. Restriction, and only by restriction, can we possibly achieve the ultimate objective of receiving.[151]

Consequently, to the extent of that state of consciousness in which we consider that we possess some form of control, to that degree of control, the Lightforce must limit and restrict Its Desire to Share.[152] The notion of conscious control limits the intensity of our own "Desire to Receive." Therefore, our ability to align with and to create a quantum connection with the Lightforce will have been greatly diminished.

The Lightforce recognizes and gauges this most important aspect of Its Desire to Share with the level and extent of our desire to receive. This connection is a serious matter and is not to be treated lightly or misrepresented. If we can achieve a consciousness of total inability to control, we have then mastered our destiny and infused our future with the beneficence of the Lightforce.[153]

The flaws and serious mistakes that continue to plague us when planning our future will no longer occur. We have simply moved into the Tree of Life consciousness where chaos and disorder do not exist. The paradox: By resisting the Lightforce in time of need and expanding our desire-to-receive consciousness, we are in a position to receive the infinite Lightforce and all that It represents, namely the certainty that furnishes structure and order in our lives. Long live the paradox.

This Kabbalistic concept of praying to the Lord is a far cry from the conventional interpretation of prayer. Theologians claim prayer is significant because it provides the healing relaxation effects that come from regular prayer and meditation. Those who turn for solace to excesses of alcohol and drugs are encouraged to rely on communion with the higher power of the Lord.

Prayers conducted in most houses of worship usually rely on rote prayer. This can, and often does, become a way of avoiding communion with the Lord even while praying with the Name of the Lord. Thus prayer, by and within itself, can lead one to complacency, thinking an action of communion has taken place and a spiritual experience is expected, when in reality, an illusionary, nonconscious connection has been established.

Others pray at moments of crisis — economic distress, a member of the family is sick or death approaches. But those who pray only at such moments usually experience greater difficulty if the miracle is not forthcoming. Then, we have those who strike a bargain with the Lord, promising to be generous in giving charity upon the request being fulfilled.

Needless to say, for the most part, we seldom hear of miracles taking place in proportion to the number of requests made. Of course, prayer does not necessarily take the form of requests. There are those who simply seek the comfort of knowing that the Lord is at their side. Or, they feel comfortable with a companion with whom they can communicate in full confidence or invoke a feeling of compassion.

However, as mentioned previously, our desire to have communion with the Lord requires much more than "desire." The connection with the Lightforce is the essential ingredient. The intense interest in prayer has been phenomenal. The edition of *Books in Print* lists over 2,000 titles on prayer, indicating a renewed intimacy with the Lord. Many have found that praying to the Lord might even have saved their life or decreased the symptoms of stress to the extent of experiencing physiological rejuvenation.

Thus, we can conclude that there are disagreements as to what prayer really is. More significantly what is the objective in prayer and what are we to expect as a result of our prayers?

Some meditative techniques claim that the practice of their meditation is imaging which induces an image in the mind's eye and contains it there. Here the image is fixed in the mind as if it were engraved. Thus, it can be held in the mind as long as one desires.

The difficulty, they claim, is achieving control over our thought process. When reading an interesting and stimulating article, close your eyes and most probably there will appear lights and images flashing before your eyes. These lights or images will come and go with no direction by the conscious mind. One image streams into another, like lakes into rivers. It is impossible to concentrate on these images, because the moment we try to inject our conscious mind they disappear.

Therefore, one of the goals of this meditation is to achieve control over the subconscious mind. It is hoped that with sufficient practice we will gain a high degree of mastering our destiny. Supposedly by claiming control over the subconscious as well as the conscious mind, this process will lead to the ultimate state of "master of our destiny and captain of our ship."

The most serious mistake made by practitioners of this meditation is to think that by gaining control of the unconscious we then gain control of the conscious mind. The assumption is that once the subconscious becomes accessible to the conscious mind, we then control the entire thought process.

The problem with this conclusion is that we cannot theorize about the conscious or subconscious mind when so little is known of either. There are innumerable theories about the subconscious, and a full discussion of this matter has been extensively provided in *To the Power of One.*[154] However, what seems so strikingly clear from a Kabbalistic perspective is that meditation or prayer does not imply controlled thinking. Even the experienced meditator will never achieve within the thought process, conscious or subconscious, the ability to think when he wants to think or think what he wants to think.

Meditation *by and within itself* cannot bring control over ourselves or achieve self-mastery over the three basic components of a happy and joyous life, namely health, wealth, and relationships. These goals, for us to enjoy, require a connection with and control by the quantum effect of the Lightforce.

In the new emerging effect of quantum physics, one eat-ing rice in China can affect every part of the globe. Today, with the world shrinking in time, space, and motion, world economic conditions inevitably must affect every global aspect of finances. If the world suffers from material or psychological chaos, every inhabitant on planet earth must be affected to a greater or lesser degree.

When we consider the notion of "control," the individual meditator must consider the possibility of an onrushing tide of disaster. Natural disasters or a complete breakdown of governments must, of necessity, affect its inhabitants. While the meditator may react in a calmer state of consciousness, nevertheless, can he control the environment when all around is crumbling? He must still rely on those two familiar words of "lucky" or "unlucky." If he is a victim then his reflection is one who has been "unlucky." If he is counted among the survivors, then he will react with the expression of being "lucky."

Lucky or unlucky has no part in, nor is it connected with, the idea of control. When we address the idea of control, then the individual must be certain that while all around is crumbling, he will manage to survive.

Consequently, in Kabbalah the goal of Kavanah Meditation is to regain total control over our lives. This major and important aspect can only be achieved by our connection to the Tree of Life reality.[155] Within this universe the Lightforce is in total control. Just what does this mean?

Kavanah means "intention" or "direction." Both prayer and meditation need to be done with *Kavanah*. The intention in both prayer and meditation is to let the ever-present Light be in our awareness. The direction is toward the limitless realm beyond the ego. Although the words of prayer are secondary, they are not redundant. Just as the soul needs the body to express itself in physical existence, so does consciousness need the Hebrew words and letters.

When the Lightforce reigns supreme there is no room for chaos and disorder to be coexistent. The seed or root of all the varied flaws found in our journey through life originates within the Tree of Knowledge reality where good and evil exist side by side. When communion with the Lightforce is established, the degree of chaos and disorder will be decreased to the extent of our connection

The ultimate goal of Kavanah Meditation is a total *Dvekut* or attachment to the Lightforce. At the Tree of Life level of reality, quantum control pervades the entire universe for those achieving a total communion with the Lightforce and, thus, taking a quantum leap into the Tree of Life universe reality.

Let us now explore a further in-depth penetration of the Tree of Life universe reality where flaws, chaos and even death simply do not exist. A good starting point for our investigation is the following striking section of the Zohar, whose declaration on the surface appears to be contradictory and almost irreconcilable. The Zohar states:[156]

> THE DAYS OF ISRAEL DREW NEAR TO DIE.[157] Rabbi Hizkiah said: Observe the difficulty of the exile that shall befall his children. This drew near to his spirit and thus his spirit was shortened to die. This is what is meant by the verse, "And the days of Israel drew near to die and he no longer could remain alive."

The preceding Zohar discusses the events that drew near

the death of Israel (Jacob) and consequently he did not remain alive. What seems apparent from the verse and the Zohar is that Israel (Jacob) did indeed die.

Upon further exploration we discover another section in the Zohar[158] which appears to contradict both the Zohar and the aforementioned verse.

> When Jacob had concluded the commands to his sons, he drew his feet back into the bed, expired and was gathered to his people.[159]

> Since he was abiding in the place of the living, [the chariot of *Zeir Anpin*, the outer space connection, the Tree of Life universe] when he was about to depart from the world [the Tree of Knowledge universe] he gathered his feet unto the bed.

What this means is that he elevated the female companion to a union with the outer space connection (*Zeir Anpin*).

Therefore the verse designates the expression "and he was gathered to his people" and does not mention the word "death" because he ascended to the upper life reality of the Tree of Life.

Jacob did not die. See what is stated: "And he drew his feet to the bed" (the female counterpart). This means the sun (Jacob) was gathered to the moon, the female counterpart. For the sun does not die, but rather is gathered from the visible, physical world and goes to the moon.

Just as in the evening the light of the sun does not leave this world, but rather "infuses" its light with the moon, so it was with Jacob when he departed from the physical world; he ascended as the unifier of the Tree of Life reality. Combining *Nukvah* (the female counterpart, *Malkhut*, the Tree of Knowledge) with *Zeir Anpin* (the Tree of Life reality where only Good[160] dominates), he infused the female counterpart of *Zeir Anpin* and his light never became nullified, and therefore, he did not die.

Praiseworthy is the portion of Jacob, for he was complete both in the upper and lower universes. Thus it is written, "And you, do not fear my servant, for with you am I."[161] The verse does not say, for with me you are. This indicates that the upper universe descends and is complete with the lower worlds to dwell upon the *Shekhinah* (the universal consciousness).

The apparent irreconcilability of the two sections in the Zohar is startling. Either Jacob died or he did not. However upon further examination of the Zoharic interpretation of "Jacob was gathered to his people" the Zohar reveals that within our universe there exists two realms of existence.

Comparing the death of Jacob to the sun weaving into the nightfall is one of the most profound thoughts appearing in the entire Zohar. The idea that the sun, after setting at any one destination, is largely due to the physical rotation of the earth does not concur with the Zohar.

When we were children, the idea that on cloudy days the sun did not shine later proved to be false once we discovered that flying above the clouds, the sun, at its appointed hour would shine whether we observed it or not.

So it is with the sun setting, states the Zohar. The sun is "gathered" and no longer infuses that particular section of the earth where nightfall begins. The Zohar engages in an *energy* discussion, the root of all physical, earthly activity. What came first, the cause or effect? In all instances, thought energy-intelligence of the human brain precedes the resulting effect manifested by the physical reality.[162] This rule is one of many natural laws that govern our universe.

Consequently, when we consider the phenomenon of nightfall, the Zohar departs from the usual, conventional explanation that our earth obstructs the light of the sun, and therefore, night time descends upon us. The physical, illusionary reality realm can never serve as a cause, justification or the responsible energy-intelligence for a physically manifested state of reality. The cause, of necessity following the laws and principles of our universe, begins by and within the metaphysical thought energy-intelligence realm of existence.

The consciousness and thought-provoking internal energy-intelligence of the sun directs and determines when nightfall descends upon us and not the physical interrelationship between sun and earth, states the Zohar. The physical interconnectedness between our sun and earth reacts and is a direct result of the sun's internal expression of its energy-intelligence.

When the Zohar decodes the death of Jacob by interpreting the word "gathering" rather than the demise of Jacob, the Zohar reveals for us a startling truth concerning the internal energy-intelligence of the sun. Unlike the accepted, scientific version concerning the sun's physical interaction with the earth as the reason behind the notion of nightfall, the Zohar's definition relates to the internal thought process of the sun.

Just as in the evening, the Light of the sun does not leave this world, but rather infuses its light within the moon.[163]

What the Zohar reveals here is that the sun ceases to reveal and bestow its own light at nightfall. The moon, the lesser of the two lights now becomes the channel for the sun's light. The sun does not directly bestow its beneficence of light upon earth. The moon serves as a conduit for the lesser light, so decreed on the fourth day of creation.[164]

While to the physical science researcher, the physical interaction relationship between earth and sun appears to explain away the phenomenon of nightfall, nevertheless, we must at the same time, consider the other side of the coin when considering physical background explanations. We must carefully examine what these same scientists have to say concerning the physical reality.

In 1927, the famous physicist, Neils Bohr, ended once and for all the classical idea of objectivity and the physical reality. No longer would the idea prevail that the world had a definitive state of existence independent of our observation. The Copenhagen Interpretation of that year maintained that at the subatomic level the world we see depends on how we *choose to see*. The indeterminism of the subatomic or quantum world implied that the traditional scientist's so-called "objective" view of physical phenomena would have to be replaced by a new observer-created perspective of reality.

Therefore, the physical world is an illusion; the real world is one step beyond. "The chair is not a chair until we observe and see it. The chair does not exist until we acknowledge that it does exist," declares the scientist. However, for most people who inhabit earth, the robotic programming of our youth determines that this idea is too far out, or most of us simply reject it outright.

To comprehend the nature of the physical world it is imperative that we begin making perceptual connections with the metaphysical realm. By the same token, to understand the nature of the external world, it is necessary to connect with the internal.

Just because something is seen with the eyes does not mean that it exists any more than not seeing something is proof that it does not exist. Through Kabbalah we peel away the layers

of illusion so that we may connect to the Light within.[165]

The idea that the sun at nightfall disappears may have contained some validity before the twentieth century. Prior to the advent of the twentieth century scientific revolution, illusion meant an incorrect perception of external stimuli. Mirages, stationary lights which seem to move in an advertisement display or when a straight spoon appears to bend when submerged in a glass of water are some familiar examples of illusion.

However, since the uncertainty principles became established as an integral component of perception, the foregoing examples do not necessarily lead to false beliefs or conclusions. Illusion no longer seems to arise from or through distorted transmission of external stimuli.

What is perceived by the individual may in essence be considered reality, and what most of us perceive as reality may in fact be connected to the false impression of the illusionary world. Quantum physics has taught us that nature's elemental properties defy objective evaluation. The immediate effect of uncertainty is that there is a "real" domain beyond. Only that man with his present limitations is not capable of entering that domain.

What seems to emerge from the preceding Zohar is the potential dual activity that appears to be present in all energy-intelligent activity. For most of us, the sun has disappeared at nightfall. For the Kabbalist, and the student trained in the study of Kabbalah, the sun did not disappear, rather it is ever present. Its disappearance is not related to its physical appearance. The sun at an appointed time discontinues its intrinsic characteristic of sharing its beneficence. The lesser light, the moon must be given the opportunity to act as a conduit of light.[166] The darkness is a direct result of the sun's ceasing to shed its light on earth.

The physically manifested interaction between the earth and the sun is an illusionary activity which has no bearing or effect on the sun as to its appearance (daybreak) or disappearance (nightfall) concerning the light of the sun.

We shall now return to the subject of whether Jacob died or is indeed alive. With the foregoing explanation regarding the sun and the moon, we now approach a reconciliation between the two contradictory verses concerning the death of Jacob.

The physical reality of burial, the notion that within the Cave of Makhpelah[167] lies the body of Jacob, the Patriarch, is considered an illusion. Inasmuch as nature's elemental properties such as sand, wood, metal, films and other physical components *defy objective evaluation*, who is to say that Jacob was buried under the earth. Possibly, Jacob is alive and well. What the observers at Jacob's so-called funeral might have witnessed is a curtain of physical realty, the earth, creating and casting the illusion that Jacob lies buried now beneath the earth.

When David Copperfield created the disappearance of the Statue of Liberty or the vanishing the Boeing 747, we became aware of the fact that it was the audience that was receding from view. The Statue of Liberty and Boeing 747 never moved from their designated position. The *audience* experienced the sensation and illusion of departure. The observer had a disappearing consciousness and thus saw these physical entities vanish before his very eyes.

Consciousness, not science, religion, or public opinion, is the harbinger of what is to come. There is no disappearance in Spiritual Substance. Nothing of value disappears. Jacob did not disappear. Even his physical body, completely unified with his spiritual substance, did not undergo any departure from our physical realm.

For those who feel a detachment from Jacob have succumbed to the illusionary consciousness of our physical reality.

Nothing of value disappears. Shapes change, the body changes, but the energy-intelligence never diminishes. The illusion changes constantly, but the truth beneath the illusion is constant and never-varying. Each stage of biological, social, and cultural evolution is impressed into the collective consciousness.

Nothing is lost. No great truths fall irretrievably between the cracks of existence. According to Kabbalistic wisdom, the physical world is just a blip on the endless screen of reality. The illusionary realm is a temporary static disruption, a pattern of interference which has existed only for the flash of the instant that we have lived as physical entities, and will be here only until that time, — the end of the process of correction — when the universe fine-tunes itself out of existence, the universal consciousness of Messiah.

Illusions are essential impediments to awareness. Words are illusions, but they often tell the truth. Books are illusions — letters, sentences, paragraphs — are channels, nothing more, and yet they have the ability to arouse our curiosity, sharpen our intellect, and more importantly to lead us to a higher state of consciousness and greater awareness of ourselves.

Music is illusion, but the emotions that it can arouse are real. Our bodies, like Jacob's, are illusions in the sense that they reveal nothing of the Infinite Energy-Intelligence within, and yet, we are also the personification of Infinity. The whole world is an illusion, and yet, it embraces a hidden aspect of reality. It is the Kabbalist's task, ultimately, to connect to this concealed Infinite phase.

The Lightforce, the Tree of Life reality is there in all of its infinite glory, but obscured from our "view" here in the illusionary realm. The universe appears to be full of violent activity. To the Kabbalist, violent phenomena are simply expressions of human violence.

"Good and evil"[168] apply to the Tree of Knowledge universe. However, the Kabbalistic journey can prepare us for entrance into the realm of the Tree of Life consciousness where chaos and disorder will be recognized for what they are — an illusion. Kabbalah teaches us the way to remove ourselves from the spiritually impoverishing cycle of negativity, struggle, failure and ultimate defeat. The quantum prayer leads us to the realm of the Tree of Life.

I recognize that the thoughts presented here are revolutionary. Coming to grips with these seemingly outlandish notions does tax the imagination. Yet, only when we fully grasp this viewpoint, can we begin to approach the study of meditation. The first step in this kind of self-healing, an integral part of the study of Kabbalah, must include the individual's recognition that he or she must consciously participate in the understanding of the makeup of the interaction between the Infinite realm of the Lightforce and its counterpart, the illusionary physical realm.

Knowledge is the connection. What we do not "know" is that with which or with whom we have not yet made contact. "Adam knew Eve and she conceived and bore Cain."[169] An obvious difficulty with this verse of the Biblical cosmic Code is, How can the mere act of knowing create a pregnancy?

The Zohar[170] explains this simply as the difference between information and knowledge. Knowledge *is* the connection. Knowledge is energy-intelligence. Obviously, there was an act of physical intercourse between Adam and Eve, states the Zohar. But why does the Bible make use of the word knowing to indicate sexual intercourse when other suitable words in Hebrew are available? The verse in Genesis states that when there is knowledge, then a direct contact has been established.

Knowledge, as I previously mentioned, is essential for the prayer techniques of Kabbalah. It is for this reason that I have written so extensively about the basic techniques. Kabbalistic techniques make demands upon its practitioners. But then again, from a Kabbalistic perspective of our world, we were never destined to behave as anything more than a complex mechanistic living organism.

What seems to have emerged thus far is the necessity of quantum connection. Any meditation that does not include or embrace the quantum events of our universe simply does not contain a quantified control of all events.

The route to the new physics of the future lies *beyond* the dimensions of the physical reality of our world. It will permit us to go beyond space-time in our analysis, and hopefully, "one day a door will open, no wider than the eye of a needle, and unto us shall open the supernal gates exposing the glittering interrelatedness (quantum feature) of the future of the universe with all its beauty and simplicity."[171]

The supernal gates lead us to the Tree of Life reality. A prayer falling short of the connection to the Tree of Life reality does not, nor can it provide quantum control. Anything less than quantum control, must of necessity drag us down to the Tree of Knowledge illusionary realm of good and evil. There, the forces of stability and certainty elude the practitioner.

Only, and I repeat, *only* a prayer that provides the meditator with communion with the Tree of Life reality guarantees the practitioner entrance to stability and certainty for his or her existence. The earth used to bury Jacob was an illusionary blackout of Jacob's existence. He did not die. He merely transformed and teleported his physical body to the realm of Tree of Life. There, death does not exist, as evidenced by the event of "Revelation on Mount Sinai."[172]

This idea concerning the stringent requirements to achieve communion with the Tree of Life reality of existence has already been expressed in the Zohar:

> In your compendium, Rabbi Shimon bar Yoḥai, the Zohar, the Book of Splendor, shall Israel and the entire world in the future taste from the Tree of Life. The Zohar, the Book of Splendor shall permit the world to go forth from its exile with Mercy.[173]

The Book of Splendor provides a direct link and contact with the universal quantum energy-intelligence that we discussed previously. The question that might now be going through the mind of my reader is, "how can I connect with and make use of the Zohar? I haven't the faintest idea how to read the material. And even if I could read the Hebrew letters, I don't have the faintest idea what it means."

Computer science has relegated the mind of mankind to a state of consciousness beneath or below the intelligence of computers. This raises a serious problem. The Kabbalah, and more particularly the Zohar, has been for too long a jealously guarded secret. However, the age of Aquarius is a *time* for the Zohar finally to come to teach the masses its message of simplicity. Because in the final analysis, knowledge understood by the layman is to be considered true knowledge.

The *future* the Zohar refers to is here and now. The Zohar elsewhere states:

> Alas for the world when Rabbi Shimon shall depart, and the fountains of wisdom will be closed. The world shall seek wisdom, there will be none to impart it. The Bible, the universal code, shall be interpreted erroneously because there will be none who is acquainted with wisdom.

> Said Rabbi Yehudah: The Lord will one day reveal to them hidden mysteries of the bible, namely, at the time of the Messiah, the Age of Aquarius, because the earth shall be full of knowledge of the Lord like the waters cover the sea.[174]

The Zohar here expresses the idea that the Messianic era will usher in a period of unprecedented enlightenment. Messianism, representing the essence of hope and optimism is bound up and dependent upon true knowledge the sublime wisdom of the Kabbalah.

The Zohar[175] states:

> In the days of the Messiah there will no longer be the necessity for one to request of his neighbor teach me wisdom, as it is written[176], "One day they will no longer teach every man his neighbor and every man his brother, saying know the Lord. For they shall all know Me, from the youngest to the oldest of them."

What the Zohar clearly expresses here is that the Messianic era will usher in a period of unprecedented enlightenment. Quantum knowledge will become available to the young and old alike as a direct result of the Aquarian era which will act as the cause of the sudden arrival of a period filled with enlightenment. The idea of twentieth century quantum knowledge was and is no accident. The seed of knowledge and enlightenment is the Messianic era which became manifested with knowledge unprecedented since the time of Shimon bar Yoḥai and his Zohar.

Messianism is the objective of the Messianic era. When a universal consciousness of total knowledge and perfection, peace and harmony are achieved, a universal Messiah-consciousness will make its appearance. The Desire to Receive for the Self Alone will be converted into Desire to Receive for the Sake of Sharing.

Scanning of the Zohar, at the very least, combines the energy-intelligence of its Aramaic writing with the computer- like mind. Our mind most certainly must equal if not surpass the ability of a product code bar scanner in departments stores. The conscious mind activates the dormant Tree of Life consciousness in our minds in the scanning process of the Zohar.

Energized by the energy-intelligence of the Zohar, our mind computers then tap the certainty paradigm of our universe. The results are astonishing. Because of the effect of mankind's limitations and the inherent prejudices into which we are born, the present collective universal consciousness affords very little opportunity for mankind to achieve a quantum positive attitude. The universal scanning of the Zohar, together with Kabbalistic meditation will hopefully foster a more cosmically positive level of thought energy-intelligence.

A commitment to self-knowledge and self-improvement

is the first requirement for anyone who wishes to take control of his life and alter his destiny if necessary. Once that commitment is made, the results can be immediate and fulfilling. Not only will we be happier in the quest to elevate our souls, but in addition we will find that pursuit of this goal begins to alleviate a great deal of the suffering initially dictated by a *Tikune*[177] pattern. It is unfortunate that it usually takes us far more lifetimes to complete a *Tikune* than might be required if we were to grasp the Tree of Life reality through quantum prayer.

Another developing channel necessary to achieve communion with the Tree of Life reality of existence is the connection gained through the listening and reading of the Biblical scroll on Saturday, Monday and Thursday. The misconception and corruption surrounding the objective and purpose of the Biblical scroll has become so prevalent in mainstream Judaism that this intimate experience has become an insignificant segment of worship.

The importance of Biblical reading has been relegated to a position of just another precept and an opportunity to earn some more points when we come face to face with our Maker. There is no indication or emphasis placed on the unique importance of the Scroll vis-a-vis the listener other than the Scroll is something very Holy, inasmuch as the Scroll was presented to the Israelites on Mount Sinai at the time of Revelation. The notion of Revelation has been all but misconstrued to mean the Lord revealed Himself to the Israelites. Just what did this mean? Very little if anything has been offered to clarify the true essence of this most important event.

From a Kabbalistic perspective, Revelation provided an opportunity for mankind to connect with the proper tools and channels in achieving communion with the Tree of Life reality and the Lightforce. The Lightforce is capable of removing the illusion of corporeal reality, the Tree of Knowledge reality, thus revealing a cosmic model that is, was, and always will be, timeless and full of certainty. This was the phenomenon of Revelation.

Unfortunately, the Israelites could not harness the awesome power of the Lightforce *revealed* by the Revelation of the Tree of Life reality. They eventually perished in the wilderness. This event occurred simply because they permitted their level of spirituality to descend. Consequently, they became the natural victims of suffering through the subsequent centuries of diaspora, persecution, inquisition, and eventually the nightmare of the holocaust.

However, with the assistance and support of the Aquarian Age, Biblical Scroll reading takes on a new significance that was not readily accessible to earlier generations. Religion, once the backbone of a vibrant civilization, has failed dismally to keep pace with the changing times.

Revelation was not and is not a one shot deal. In each generation, we must return to the revealment of the Tree of Life reality if we are to secure sanity and order in our lives. The Kabbalistic dictum of "no loss, no disappearance in spirituality" denotes that the Revelation event exists for us today. We have at our disposal the Time Machine[178] which provides our traveling back in time to permit our presence again at Mount Sinai and Revelation.

The prayer of *Be'rikh Shemei*[179] is the Zoharic Time Machine. Once we have traveled back in time to Revelation, the reading and listening of the Biblical scroll provides the opportunity of tapping the awesome power of the Tree of Life reality.

Said Rabbi Shimon: When the Scroll is removed

from the Ark for the purpose of public reading,
the Gates of Heaven of Raḥamim are opened,[180]
initiating and arousing the Love of Above [the All
embracing Unified Whole — the Tree of Life
reality] and then man should say the following
Be'rikh Shemei.

The universe appears to be full of violent activity. To the
Kabbalist, violent phenomena are simply expressions of human
violence. Good and evil apply to the Tree of Knowledge universe.
However, the Kabbalistic journey, the *Be'rikh Shemei* and reading
of the Biblical Scroll can prepare us for entrance into the realm of
the Tree of Life consciousness, where chaos and disorder will be
recognized for what they are — an illusion. The Scroll provides us
with the way to remove ourselves from the spiritually impoverishing cycle of negativity, struggle, failure and ultimate defeat.

The Zoharic Time Machine provides the transportation
to travel back in time to the event of Revelation. This may come
as a surprise to many of the readers of this volume. How and
where do we connect with an event that is now considered history? That occasion is but a recorded memory for many Bible
adherents. The event has descended down to our century as a tradition, a holiday celebration as any other contemporary national
holiday.

However, with a Kabbalistic perspective concerning
Biblical events, the Biblical occurrences exist in the present as in
the past and those of the future. Scientists today are discovering a
whole array of new phenomena, many of which have taken us
from the familiar material world that belongs to human experience to a signpost pointing to a more complex view of reality.

Time and space, objectively speaking, have almost vanished in the paranormal, the worlds of metaphysics, along a path strewn with paradoxes and strange phenomena. These Biblical incidents all suggest concepts and things, and *not tradition* or *religion*; ideas that will hopefully be rediscovered leading eventually to a redefinition of reality in a way that all mankind shall understand and see.

The journey pursued in these pages has been an attempt to track down the cosmic power sources of the Tree of Life reality. The event of Revelation exists in the here and now, along with the other events which are included within the cosmic calendar and timetable. In other words, we cannot choose our own timetable, no less than we can alter the time schedule of a television guide to programming.

The Biblical events and so-called Jewish holidays are the precise indication when we can tap the cosmic power of our universe, the Tree of Life universe. More importantly, the coded instructions of the so-called Jewish holidays are the methods and channels by which we embark upon and make the cosmic connection journey. Once the cosmic connection has been bonded in unity with the Tree of Life universe, we have crossed the threshold of strange phenomena, where past, future and present combine to become unified. Once we gain admittance, Revelation becomes a present event for revealing the Lightforce.

All such holidays and festivals are merely time frames because the naked eye certainly never will observe astrological and cosmological influences stemming from them. Consequently, what has been provided in that mass of words called the Bible is merely the timetable of what and when cosmological events are taking place and what forces they bring to hand.

Nearly all who "pray" in good faith, whether Jew, Moslem

or Christian, will testify that their prayers are frequently answered. However, few, if any of them know why. How much more powerful their prayers would be if they did.

Let us explore one of the festivals mentioned in the Bible and examine the Kabbalistic perspective of its meaning. The Biblical festival related to Revelation on Mount Sinai is known as Shavuot or Pentecost, the feast of harvest.[181]

The superficial or conventional interpretation of this festival is the time when the first-fruits are brought to the sanctuary or Holy Temple. The first and obvious question that must be raised is wherein lies the relationship between Revelation and this festival? How does the idea of first-fruits connect to Revelation? Here is another apparent dogmatic doctrine which leaves the observer in the dark, and brings about a robotic style of religion where the participating individual is instructed to act and perform this precept without receiving any answers to these glaring questions.

However, when Rabbi Isaac Luria defines this event as an opportunity to purchase and acquire "life insurance," the entire concept takes on new meaning. Incidently, I am not referring to the "life insurance" that we have become familiar with. The "life insurance" that requires the purchaser to first die before one can reap the benefits of "life insurance." How odd and peculiar is our notion of life insurance. We might assume that we were acquiring a right to extend our life. Or perhaps, that we have some inalienable right to prevent death from inflicting its horrible consequences on mankind.

However, we are well aware of the conventional interpretation of the meaning of life insurance. There are reasons why insurance companies refer to their product as "life insurance" and not "death insurance," which is the truthful designation of the product. Because, let's face it, who would buy a product referred to as "death insurance"?

Let us now return to the Kabbalistic claim that it is possible to acquire immunity from the chaos known as death. For most of us, this statement smacks of quackery and breeds of charlatanism. Frankly, if I were exposed to these kinds of claims, I too would turn a deaf ear. In fact, before my entrance into the world of Kabbalah, the notion of paranormal phenomena was an idea that could not fit into the mainstream. Tunnel vision was the order of the day.

How surprised I was to discover that Kabbalah, with a recorded history of 3,800 years, devoted the major writings to the reality level of the Tree of Life. As a matter of fact, the above-mentioned claim is stated in the Zoharic text and Rabbi Isaac Luria's discourse on meditation.

The Zohar states the following:[182]

Come, dear friends, come and let us renew the preparations of the bride in this night (Shavuot). For everyone who remains awake all night with her will be guarded and shielded throughout the year, above and below, and complete the year in peace.

It is of them that it is written: "The angel of the Lord encamps around those who fear him and delivers them from danger. Taste and see that the Lord is good."[183]

With the Zohar's striking and startling revelation, the

idea of connection to the certainty and order of the Tree of Life universe becomes a reality. The certainty of an extension to our expected life span seems incredulous. Never before has such an idea been presented except possibly the search for the Fountain of Youth.

Death and taxes are considered the only two certainties in our civilization. The contrary notion, suggested by the Zohar some two thousand years ago, will certainly find acceptance hard to come by, if not outright rejection.

However, once we have acquired the knowledge of parallel universes — the Tree of Life and the Tree of Knowledge of Good and Evil — our expanded awareness and consciousness should assist us in reaching the point of embracing new phenomena of the paranormal. Most of earth's inhabitants have witnessed the few who have provided us with new inventions and discoveries. They have never been participating players in the unfoldment of the Age of Aquarius. They have never taken an active role in the Aquarian scenario.

In the twentieth century alone, science has completely abandoned much of the antiquated ideas that have formed the attitude and perspective of our universe. Its acceptance by the rest of mankind was slow in coming. In our day and age, the scientific ideas that have literally changed the thinking and behavior of the masses still remain a mystery and, at their very least, unintelligible to most of us.

Mankind has always left the responsibility to others, whether it be government, politicians, doctors or physicists. The mind is rusty for lack of initiative. However, with the arrival of the Age of Aquarius, the twentieth century has been a witness to a people's attempt to express themselves and take matters into their control, a people's revolution where government and other organizations no longer are to be considered the experts over our lives. The decision to seek another medical opinion, or take control of our environment, while slow in coming, has become a reality.

The Age of Aquarius has literally coerced us into rethinking our priorities and actions. An example of this change in attitude is the "nineties" condemnation of excesses in the eighties. Reviewing our behavior has never been the trademark of humankind. There was always someone out there that could be blamed for our chaos and misery. The people's revolution in overthrowing incompetent governments without a single shot being fired has never been the trademark of conflicts. Bloodless revolutions, no matter how dictatorial the government, have become commonplace.

In most cases, the reason behind this phenomenon has been the "desire to receive for oneself alone." Nevertheless, there is every indication that people will now begin to express themselves, rather than assume passive action and commitments.

The New Age scientific findings have long been expressed by the Kabbalists, the only difference being that the Kabbalist touched base with the Tree of Life reality. Thus, they perceived the future journey of mankind. The people were not prepared, nor were they willing, to consider these new ideas. Mankind would have to wait for an understanding of the Biblical code. The Kabbalah provided the unraveling of universal mysteries. But, without the dawn of Aquarius, the Kabbalists' decoding remained abstruse and concealed.

Science was necessary in the process of raising the consciousness of the people. But this too awaited Aquarian awareness. Rabbi Ashlag was mankind's answer to a clear and precise understanding of the *Book of Formation* and the Zoharic text. We were furnished with an opportunity to understand and penetrate the activity around us. More importantly, the gnawing question of "why" could now be dealt with, whereas the answers to the essential "whys" have always eluded the scientific community.

We can *now* return to the question raised previously; how does the festival of Shavuot relate to our new-found phenomenon of controlling and extending the life cycle. One indication concerning the power of the Age of Aquarius lies in its ability to increase life expectancy. The average life span of a person born in the United States increased from approximately 39 years in 1929 to approximately 75 years in 1988, an increase of approximately 92 percent.

Sketching this concept to its extreme, the Age of Aquarius is our physical evidence that the prospect of extending our lifespan by our personal behavior and communion with the Tree of Life reality is at hand. The idea was stated in the Zohar.[184] The method and personal raising of our consciousness would have to await the Aquarian Age.

Now, why does Shavuot bring with it the opportunity to extend our life span? Let us further investigate the event known as Revelation on Mount Sinai. The significance and implication of Revelation previously noted was the Revelation of the quantum effect of the Tree of Life. The Tree of Knowledge illusionary reality, the Dark Lord and its chaos, ceased to exist, no less than darkness in a room which comes to an end through the power of illumination.

When Revelation became a quantum reality, its force brought about the demise of the concept and existence of death.

The life cycle was now restored to the manifested state of Adam prior to the Sin.[185] Adam was destined to live forever had he not eaten the apple of the Tree of Knowledge. At the moment of Revelation, states Scripture, "Death shall be eternally swallowed up"[186] If the Golden Calf incident[187] had never taken place, then death would no longer have existed within the scenario of mankind.

According to the Zohar, "all the celestial treasures and hidden mysteries that were not revealed to succeeding generations will be revealed in the Age of Aquarius."[188] It implies that this new age will provide us with a comprehension not only of our familiar universe, but of that which lies beyond the range of observation, in the realm of the metaphysical, the non-space domain.

Today, more than at any other time in history, the Lightforce is *demanding* to be revealed. "As the Lightforce of the Lord separated those on Mount Sinai, so shall He separate them at the final redemption."[189] The Revelation on Mount Sinai is interpreted by the Zohar to mean a connection between the raw energy of the Lightforce and the nation of Israel. Hence the use of the word "revelation" which means being revealed without the usual protective elements that cloak and conceal. The Aquarian Age then, will be an age of revelation.

The Ari, Rabbi Isaac Luria, considered the problems connected with the Aquarian Age. He also provided an insight into the root, which he drew from the doctrines of reincarnation.

> The generation of *Dor-Deah* [the all-knowing generation], the generation of intelligence, shall once again rise in reincarnated souls during the Age of Aquarius.[190]

The Ari demonstrates his familiarity with the internal cosmic activity and intelligence of the Aquarian Age. The *Erev Rav* is that segment of the Israelites who, at the time of the Exodus, displayed an arrogance and insensitivity that assured the failure of their mission. Persons today lacking compassion, tolerance and sensitivity for others corrupt the cosmos with their negative energy-intelligence.

It is to the *Erev Rav* Jew that we owe a world torn by violence and particularly anti-semitism. They are directly responsible for holocaust and destruction throughout the world all through the centuries. They are also incarnated souls from the generation of the Tower of Babel[191], states the Zohar.[192]

> The builders of edifices, they construct places of worship and houses of study. They dedicate scrolls of the Torah and put crowns upon the Scrolls. However, their acts are anything but altruistic. Their one purpose is to create an image and name for themselves. As it is written, "let us make for ourselves a name."[193] These individuals are boisterous, vocal and attempt to dominate those who have been blessed. Ultimately their selfish indulgence causes their places of worship and houses of study to be broken and destroyed.

The *Erev Rav* of the Exodus were incapable of completing their *Tikune* or correction in their then existing corporeal bodies. Having no choice, the Lord decreed, "Your carcasses shall fall in this wilderness all that were numbered of you, according to your whole number, from twenty years old and over, which have murmured against me."[194]

Throughout recorded history, humankind has been divided, from a Kabbalistic perspective, into two basic categories, the *Erev Rav* and the Israelites. The bloodstained history of religious conflict incorporates these two qualities. All religions are made up of both those who accept the premise of "Love thy neighbor"[195] and those who purvey the energy-intelligence of evil. Intolerance, prejudice, and bigotry in the name of the Lord are manifestations of the antisocial face of the Dark Lord, the *Erev Rav*.

Here we see the intimate connection between the Age of Aquarius and the reincarnation of the *Erev Rav*. The evil intelligence of the *Erev Rav* will become expressed in its violence as never before experienced in human history, thus the desperate necessity of quantum prayer in this Age of Aquarius.

The Zohar foresaw this traumatic age as one of extremes. In those times, states the Zohar:[196]

> Rabbi Shimon raised his hands, wept and said, *woe* unto him who meets with that period. *Praiseworthy* is the portion of him who encounters and has the divine capacity to be cast in that time.

The glaring paradox of opposites, the "woe" and "praiseworthy," at the same Messianic period is explained by Rabbi Shimon in the Zohar as follows:

> Woe unto him who meets with that period for when the Lightforce shall make contact with the Shekhinah [the channel for quantum revealment], He shall gaze upon those who stand loyal to her [connected], upon all who have become unified with her [*Shekhinah*].

The Lightforce will scrutinize the actions and deeds of each of those who are not found righteous. Upon these the Scriptures declare,[197] "I looked and there is none [*Shekhinah*] to help." For these, agonizing torment and trouble lie in wait.

Praiseworthy, however, are those who shall merit the joy-giving Lightforce, those who have become unified with the *Shekhinah*. Concerning this period "and the evils," Scriptures state, "I will refine them as silver is refined, I shall cleanse them as gold is cleansed."[198]

Rabbi Shimon affirmed that the Messianic Era will bring with it the Lightforce and a richness representing the infusion of the Lightforce through all the worlds. The dawn of a new world will appear, and with its advent the Lightforce will begin to liberate men from their ignorance, bringing them spiritual awakening and lives of well-being.[199]

This objective, declares the Zohar, is inextricably connected with *Hokhmah* (wisdom) and completely dependent upon the dissemination of true knowledge, the sublime wisdom of the Kabbalah.[200]

What seems to emerge from the Zohar is the extremely paradoxical nature of the Age of Aquarius, very similar to the period of the Exodus and the *Erev Rav*, and closely resembling the calamity taking place in the world we live in at the present.

A good part of the world has experienced freedom in a manner never equaled in the course of history since the time of the Exodus. However, a closer examination of the Exodus event reveals another side to this glorious and joyous occasion. The Israelites enjoyed and underwent dramatic changes and experiences from being a horde of slaves, to witnessing the Ten Plagues, freedom from the mighty Middle Kingdom, to the Splitting of the Red Sea. However, these incredible, miraculous events were not lasting nor convincing enough to change the internal characteristic of the *Erev Rav*.

As they approached the Red Sea and "saw the Egyptians marching after them, they were sore afraid; and the children of Israel cried out to the Lord. And they said unto Moses: Because there were no graves in Egypt, hast thou taken us away to die in the wilderness? Why have you dealt with us this way, to bring us forth out of Egypt? Is this not the word that we spoke unto thee in Egypt, saying: Let us alone, that we may serve the Egyptians? For it were better for us to serve the Egyptians, than that we should die in the wilderness."

For a nation to participate in the miraculous events of the Exodus only to turn the next day and completely forget what had occurred the day before.is mystifying. Is it indeed possible to erase so quickly from our memory events which occurred only yesterday? While we may all experience a lapse of memory from time to time, the Exodus event seems too incomprehensible to grasp.

Another example of *Erev Rav consciousness* occurs only a few weeks later following another miraculous event, the splitting of the Red Sea. It was an unusual event, and because it was so unusual, it has remained one of the most impressive cosmic upheavals in the long history of the nation of Israel.

And Moses stretched out his hand over the sea;
and the Lord caused the sea to go back by a
strong east wind all that night, and made the sea
dry land, and the waters were divided.[201]

All nations and peoples of the world experienced this enormous cosmic energy-intelligence force that instantly pervaded the entire universe, according to the Biblical commentator Rashi. Because of the grammatical structure of this verse, and as explained by the Mekhilta "the waters of all oceans and seas were divided."[202]

A cosmic upheaval of such proportions swept through every corner of the Earth and universe. The traditions of many peoples along with cosmological myth persist that seas were torn apart, "waters were piled up to the height of sixteen hundred miles and they could be seen by all the nations of the world."[203]

Indeed, an incredible event. How long would it be remembered?

> And they took their journey from Elim ... on the fifteenth day of the second month after their departure from the Land of Egypt. And the entire congregation of Israel complained against Moses and Aaron in the wilderness. And the Israelites said unto them: Would that we had died by the hand of the Lord in the land of Egypt, when we sat by the fleshpots, when we did eat bread to the full; for you have brought us forth into this wilderness, to kill this whole assembly with hunger.[204]

Throughout the bible, throughout their journey in the wilderness, we read of the *Erev Rav* as people never satisfied. In this connection, the Bible for the first time associates the word "Nazi" to the evil consciousness of the *Erev Rav* Jew.[205] Their outlook on life and personal experiences reveal their intrinsic character, one of "what have you done for me lately."

This, then, is the paradoxical nature of the Aquarian Age.

Along with the reincarnation of the *Erev Rav Jew*, the Aquarian Age must, of necessity, recreate the Revelation of Mount Sinai so as to permit the rest of mankind to survive. The knowledge of Kabbalah is and will be opposed by these evil-consciousness ridden people among us.

Indeed a startling declaration, in light of the recent holocaust in which the perpetrators of mass murder, torture and terrorism were also known as Nazis. The Ari's description and connection of the gloom of Armageddon with the Aquarian Age provides the link between chaos and human activity.

Even today, persons lacking tolerance corrupt the entire cosmos with their Armageddon negativity. The Aquarian state of affairs will become unbearable for humankind. Our only hope is to maintain our connection with the Tree of Life reality. One of the channels available in achieving communion with the Tree of Life is our journey back in time to "Revelation" on Mount Sinai, accomplished by listening to the reading of the Biblical Scroll.

The Dark Lord is fully aware of the opportunity provided by the Biblical Scroll. His efforts, during the Age of Aquarius are therefore directed towards undermining and sabotaging this instrument (Scroll). And thus mankind is prevented from making use of the most powerful vehicle available in reaching our objective, to be at one with the Lightforce.

The Zohar recognizes this danger when it discusses the Age of Aquarius and the effectiveness of the Biblical Scroll.[206]

And in the future, the world shall cry in distress, and there shall be none that pay attention to them. They shall turn their heads in all directions seeking any solution or salvation, and they shall not return with any remedy to their anguish.

However only one cure have I found in all the world, and none other, to wit, in the place where there will be people involved with Torah, and where there will be a Biblical Scroll that is not invalid. And when the Scroll is withdrawn from the Ark, there will be forthcoming a connection with and an arousal of the upper and lower dimensions. And how much more effective is this Scroll when the Holy Name is written as it should be. We have already dwelt on this matter elsewhere.

The Zohar, with its customary description concerning the Aquarian Age, reveals the importance of the Scroll, as we have previously mentioned. The Aquarian Age would be the information age where knowledge unknown for the past two thousand years would come to light. The ritual and dogmatic character associated with the reading of the Scroll would cease to be a viable religious practice. Mankind could now connect to this powerful channel as one of the pathways and ingredients of the quantum prayer. The Scroll was no longer merely a document which deserved our respect and admiration simply because the Lord found it fitting to share his beneficence and knowledge with the Israelites in the wilderness.

No! this Scroll provided a roadmap and journey by which we could abandon the Tree of Knowledge universe with its chaos and suffering. The Scroll was a time-tunnel spaceship by which we might experience the euphoria of the Tree of Life reality.

What options were available to the Dark Lord by which he could shatter our dreams in achieving a glimpse of happiness and contentment? To make certain that the Scrolls become invalid without the people being aware as to what constitutes a valid Scroll. To our dismay and confusion, the Dark Lord has almost succeeded in his mission.

The Rabbinate, aided by sophisticated scanners, estimate now that over ninety percent of all existing Scrolls are indeed invalid. Just as the Zohar had predicted some two thousand years ago. The opportunity for mankind to connect with the Tree of Life has in our Aquarian Age, been greatly diminished.

Consequently, the Exodus incarnation into the present era has already made the paradoxical nature of the people of the Exodus a reality. Today, too, hundreds of millions of people have achieved their freedom in a miraculous way. Gone are the days when freedom was accompanied with enormous bloodshed.

However, just as in the time of the Exodus, the Israelites all too soon forgot their newly acquired freedom only to protest the economic bad times, so too now the rewards of freedom in our time have all been erased and replaced by the chaos, disorder and uncertainty that followed the preceding wonderful events.

More strife and conflict have emerged from this freedom process. People no longer are concerned about the benefits to the whole community. They would rather withdraw into themselves and permit the Dark Lord to impregnate the seeds of the "desire to receive for the self alone" into the whole of the universe, almost permitting a resettling into the Tree of Knowledge reality with all its confusion and chaos.

The confusion surrounding the notion of prayer and its objectives, the scanning of the Zohar, and the reading of the Scroll is the result of the negative activity of the Dark Lord.

Prayer no longer is what it once was meant to be. Discouraging the study and dissemination of the Zohar and the absence of valid Scrolls are all manifested states of the Dark Lord.

Without the establishment of a quantum prayer consciousness, which includes multiple channels and methods, the Tree of Life reality appears to be beyond our immediate perspective and seems to be far off in the future. However, the opposite holds true for us today. This knowledge and these methods for activating the Tree of Life in our daily lives are near and quite at hand.

It remains for us to achieve a greater awareness of our inalienable rights as a people to acquire happiness and fulfillment and inject this well-being into our daily lives. The choice is not the Lord's, but rests completely on our ability to achieve an elevated state of consciousness, to understand that chaos and disorder are but illusions. The Tree of Life reality is by all means attainable and accessible.

Chapter Nine

Belief and Miracles

THE CONCEPT AND DEFINITION OF MIRACLES MAY VARY. The description of a miracle may differ from religion to religion. Then there are those miracles which a person has personally experienced. Whether this is of divine intervention or simply beyond understanding, our reaction to a supernatural occurrence is always accompanied by the thoughts of "Thank the Lord" for this miraculous event.

Then we have the "believers" for whom, in their opinion, miracles are proof that the Lord exists and is involved in our affairs. However, when chaos and misfortune become the rule, does the believer still maintain the same steadfast belief in the Lord as when a miracle occurs?

There is no intent on my part to question the beliefs of

anyone. This is a personal matter that is best left alone; nor is the intent to place in question the idea of belief. However, the question being raised at this time is whether in times threatening disaster is belief in the Lord diminished or strengthened? Have we ever found ourselves saying "Lord, where were you when I needed you?"

Before continuing our subject on miracles, there is one other significant point that must be raised concerning belief. When we employ the word "belief" we should be aware of its connotation. The word "believer" by and within itself indicates uncertainty. Or, for that matter, whenever we say "I believe" we're assuming a certain reservation. Otherwise we make use of the word I "know."

But then again, how could I "know" about the Lord when I have never come "face to face" with the Lord. Moses, following the Golden Calf incident, requested that the Lord permit him to see the Lord's face. "And He said: You cannot see My face; for no man shall see Me and live."[207] Moses desired to know what no human being can fathom, what no human language can express.

Furthermore, the Zohar[208] in its discourse on "knowing the Lord" stresses its importance and necessity.

> AND I WILL TAKE YOU TO ME FOR A PEOPLE AND I
> WILL BE TO YOU A LORD, AND YOU SHALL KNOW
> THAT I AM THE LORD YOUR LORD.[209] This is the
> first of all commandments, the root of all precepts
> of the Law, the knowledge of the Lord in a general way, namely that there is a Supernal Ruler,
> Lord of the universe and of all life, Creator of
> heaven and earth and all their hosts. But this gen-

eral knowledge of the Lord must lead on to a particular knowledge of Him.

When the Israelites were about to come out of Egypt, they had no knowledge of the Holy one. Moses had to teach them the first principles of Divine knowledge. Without this doctrine they would not have believed in all those signs and miracles which they were about to experience.

At the end of the forty years in the desert, after having been instructed by Moses in all the commandments, both in those which are directly connected with the Holy Land and in those which are not, he taught them in an individual, particular way, the knowledge of the Lord, as it says "Know therefore this day and consider it in your heart that the Lord is in heaven above and in the earth beneath; there is no one else."[210] ...Thus the whole duty of man is to know the Holy One, Blessed be He, in a general and in a particular way.

The verse, "I am the first, and I am the last"[211] has a symbolic reference to this twofold mode of knowledge; "I am the first" to the general apprehension of Him, and "I am the last" to the particular, and these two are one.

As a result of a proper knowledge of the Lord as Creator, the two hundred and forty-eight sections [bone structure] of the human body become sections of the two hundred and forty-eight positive precepts of the Torah, [man's body and soul act as channel for the healing process] and man's life becomes complete and harmonious, and the particular, individual, knowledge of the Lord causes salvation and blessings to enter into every day of the three hundred and sixty-five days of the year [corresponding to the three hundred sixty-five negative precepts]. For as it is above so is it below: as all the supernal and paranormal "days" are filled constantly with blessings by the [heavenly] Man, [the Tree of Life reality], so are the days here below [the Tree of Knowledge reality] filled with blessings through the channel of Man.[212]

What seems to emerge from this striking Zohar is that, without knowledge of the Lord, the amount and types of miracles a person will experience will *never* bring him to a belief in the Lord. This notion is a far cry from the religious conception of miracles that it surely brings the individual to a belief in the Lord. "Without this doctrine they would not have believed in all those signs and miracles which they were about to experience," making it strikingly clear, says the Zohar, that miracles alone do not reinforce belief in the Lord.

The concept presented by the Zohar is supported by another verse in Scriptures, where it states, "And Israel saw the great work which the Lord did upon the Egyptians, and the people feared the Lord; and they believed in the Lord, and in His servant Moses."[213] The "great work" referred to in the Scriptures was the splitting of the Red Sea.

However, a mere three weeks later, on the fifteenth day of the second month,[214] the moment that the need for food was experienced, the Israelites complained and in anger murmured at Moses and Aaron stating, "It would have been better had we died at the hand of the Lord in the Land of Egypt, when we sat by the flesh pots, where we ate bread to the full; for you have brought us out of Egypt into the wilderness, to kill this whole assembly with hunger."[215]

They remembered the flesh-pots and bread only, but not their slavery. This was all gone and forgotten. But then again, the event, freedom from bondage, happened so long ago, four weeks previously, to be exact. This, of course, is not to mention the miraculous "splitting of the Red Sea." After all, the Lord *now* must be *powerless* to furnish the Israelites with food.

How did the Lord respond to the Israelite complaint? "Then said the Lord unto Moses: Behold, I will cause to rain bread from heaven for you."[216] The food that the Lord will provide them with will surely save them from starvation. However, the manner in which it was given was to test their faith and belief in the Lord.

"And Moses said unto them: Let no man leave of it [the bread which was also referred to in Scriptures as Manna from heaven] until the morning."[217] Now logically, this condition certainly did not present any hardship for the Israelites. Why would Moses ever have a thought that after all the miracles and now Manna from heaven, they would still fail to have belief in the Lord? But apparently, Moses understood the human instinct in man, his animal nature of the "desire to receive for the self alone."[218] Miracles by and within themselves do not alter or change the intrinsic nature of selfish man.

Further evidence of this intrinsic nature of man is borne out by Scriptures. When the Lord requested that each person take only what was necessary for a day's consumption and no more, to indicate their belief in the Lord, they paid no heed even to this simple request.

> Notwithstanding they did not listen to Moses,
> and some of them left of it [the Manna] until the
> morning and it bred worms, and rotted; and
> Moses was filled with anger at them.[219]

Exploring this incident with an open awareness, it
becomes self evident to what extent the "evil inclination of man"
may become manifest. The *uncertainty* of whether the next day
will again bring the blessing of the Manna never left; nor does it
leave man. This, irrespective of how many of the Lord's miracles
one has been exposed to or experienced. Another illustration that
miracles neither support nor induce belief in the Lord: down to
the present hour, rejoicings like those on the shore of the Red Sea
have always been followed by murmurings like those at the
Waters of Strife.

Immediately following their despair at not having bread,
the journey of complaining began, a trademark which has never
left the Israelites to this very day. It is the nature of man to overrate
a present evil. The slaves were wonderfully set free. At the moment
of their liberation they raised a song of gratitude and triumph.[220]
But in a few hours they began to regret their freedom, and to con-
demn the leader who had lured them away from the appetizing
food of the house of bondage to the awful waste of the wilderness.

> And they encamped in Rephidim and there was
> no water for the people to drink. They wrangled
> with Moses, and said: Give us water that we may
> drink. And Moses said to them: Why do you
> argue with me? Why do you continue to test the
> Lord? And the people thirsted there for water;
> and the people murmured against Moses, and

said: Why did you bring us out of Egypt, to kill us, our children and our cattle with thirst? And Moses cried unto the Lord, saying: What shall I do for this people? They are almost prepared to stone me.....You shall strike the rock, and there shall come forth water out of it, that the people may drink.[221]

This scenario continues throughout the Bible. The unfulfilled Israelite weaves through the essential fibre of all Scripture. The miracle model presented by the Bible indicates, without doubt, the ineffectiveness of miracles to persuade or influence mankind towards a belief in the Divine. The words of the Zohar shine forth as a beacon of light in the dark, an enigmatic definition of the mystery of miracles.

The conventional and widespread meaning of miracles is that it is supposed to be something extraordinary and unpredictable. When we consider certain natural happenings, we find that this description does not fulfill the recipe for miracles. Are we to consider the eruption of volcanoes or the fall of a gigantic meteorite as fitting the description of a miracle? Most of us might well agree that, generally speaking, a miracle also contains the ingredient of "lucky," as in the survival after a serious mishap.

Such phenomena as the volcano or earthquake are natural events, known events in the nature of things. Miracles belong to the category of supernatural occurrences. Falling from a seventeenth floor window and surviving may be considered by many to be in the class of miracle. However, this attitude towards miracles then places a limitation and focuses on whether the individual becomes a victim or survivor.

Another serious problem with this definition is that we

have removed the universal concept of miracle to one of a particular, individual expression. Miracles are supernatural when the event is outside the ordinary operation of cause and effect. Then again, this depends on what one means by "ordinary."

Miracles, then, might be construed as taking place when a business which has prospered some sixty years suddenly finds itself in financial difficulties to the point of bankruptcy and then, out of nowhere, a client or customer appears who singlehandedly turns the entire business around — literally removes it from impending disaster to a level higher than was experienced over the period of sixty years. This event doesn't fit the requirement of "cause and effect." However, one might find this event out of the ordinary. Supernatural? No. Survivor? Yes.

Placed within a personal framework the notion of miracles becomes subject to individual interpretation. Whereas one might conclude that a miracle did in fact take place, others might characterize the downturn or upswing as a daily occurrence taking place somewhere in our universe. However, one thing is for certain, an atheist or irreligious person would never consider this sort of event in any way connected with Divine intervention.

Let us now turn to one of the most dramatic, miraculous events which took place during the Exodus from Egypt, the Splitting of the Red Sea.[222]

> And Moses stretched out his hand over the sea;
> and the Lord caused the sea to go back by a
> strong east wind all the night and made the sea
> dry land, and the waters were divided.

A superficial analysis of the preceding verse places into question the notion about the greatest miracle of them all, the

Splitting of the Red Sea. The Biblical description appears to give credence to the notion that this miraculous event was not as incredible as one might believe, but was rather based upon a natural cause. Miracles are usually attributed to a Divine intervention.

The verse however seems to attribute the Splitting of the Red Sea to a strong east wind, which blowing all night and reacting with the ebbing tide, might have reduced the water joining the Bitter Lakes to the Red Sea. The result of the wind permitted the Israelites to cross to safety. Consequently, the boundless power of the Lightforce appears to have played a minor roll in the event.

However, one might reason, doesn't the verse state "*the Lord caused* the sea to go back by a strong east wind," indicating Divine intervention? Nevertheless, some skeptics might still raise the question, "why did the Lord need the support of the east wind in dividing the waters?" Was it not possible for the Lord to accomplish the splitting of the sea by Himself?

Furthermore, on closer examination of the verse, we also take notice of the Lord instructing Moses to intervene in the miracle process. "...and lift up thy rod [staff] and stretch out thy hand over the sea, and divide it; and the children of Israel shall go into the midst of the sea on dry ground."[223]

Within the verse just mentioned there is not the slightest indication that there was any further necessity of intervention beyond the action of Moses splitting the sea — neither the Lord causing, nor an east wind making the sea to turn to dry land and dividing the waters.

One verse, gives the impression that it was the rod of

Moses that split the sea. The later verse indicates the intervention of both the Lord and the strong east wind.

Before our very eyes, the splitting of the Red Sea turns from the notion of a simple, miraculous event recorded in the Bible to one of confusion, and develops into an incomprehensible wonder. Really frustrating. Might we not be better off just to leave things as they are? Most are of the opinion that ignorance is bliss. However, let us never forget even for a moment, that ignorance is not, nor ever will be, a deterrent towards a future of uncertainty.

Only with *knowledge* can we embark upon a journey of structure and order in our lives. The certainty of tomorrow comes to those connected with the Lightforce and the Tree of Life reality. Its pathways are encoded within the superficial meanings of the Bible. The Kabbalah deciphers and decodes the message. No longer do we have to be content with the superficial level of Scriptures.

Yes, this does involve acquiring Kabbalistic knowledge and information for which a conscious effort must be made and time spent. However, the rewards and compensation for the painstaking and laborious investment are well worth it. To many of us, the trouble and stress may require a transformation within our consciousness. As difficult as it may appear during the process, the contentment and certainty that germinate and follow from our determination to be in communion with the Lightforce will more than compensate for those far and in-between illusionary obstacles placed in our path.

Many relationships will undergo inevitable changes. Ignorance will appear as a more desirable option. But if we merely devote a little time in observing our existing relationships, financial environment and the health climate, we shall assuredly come away with a feeling that we have only two options. To choose ignorance and its accompanying uncertainties in our daily life, or to opt for the Lightforce and Tree of Life reality which provides stability and a future of certainty.

However, cautions the Zohar, the pathway to the Tree of Life reality is strewn with obstacles, the reason being to require man to make an effort to overcome the stumbling blocks along the journey to the Tree of Life. Otherwise, mankind would find no reward in its trip. It would be deserving of the consequences bound up with the doctrine of Bread of Shame.[224]

> Said Rabbi Abba: How many thousands, how many myriads, of celestial cohorts surround the Lightforce. Lords of sharp weapons, lords of the piercing cry, lords of the heralding trumpet, lords of mercy, lords of judgment.
>
> Above them the Lord has appointed the Matrona [*Malkhut*] to minister before Him in the Palace. She for her own bodyguard has armed hosts of sixty different degrees. Holding their swords, they stand around Her. They come and go, entering and departing again on the errands of their Master. Each with his six wings outspread, they circle the world in swift and silent flight.
>
> Before each of them, coals of fire burn. Their garments are woven of flames from a bright and burning fire. A sharp flaming sword also is at the shoulder of each to guard Her. Concerning these words it is written: "The flaming sword which turned every way to guard the way of the Tree of

Life!"225

Now, what is the path of the Tree of Life? This is the great Matrona [*Shekhinah-Malkhut*] who is the way to the great and mighty Tree of Life....

Every message which the King wishes to send out is sent through the Matrona, and conversely, every message sent from the lower spheres to the King. Thus, the Matrona is the messenger between the upper regions and the lower.226

The Zoharic text makes this point strikingly clear. Achieving communion with the Lightforce is no easy task. It is like running an obstacle course. In the absence of an intense effort and knowledge of what awaits the runner, he is unlikely to reach the finishing line. Similarly, mankind, in the endeavor to actualize stability and order along the journey of life, requires a commitment to reach the Tree of Life reality. However, there can be no success in this undertaking unless there is an acceptance of the responsibility to *know*.

This heretofore unknown gateway to a manifested state of certainty and assurance of mastery over matters pertaining to health, wealth and relationships must, of necessity, harmonize with the effort put forward. The rewards of the Tree of Life are so profound and all encompassing. To assume that we may acquire these benefits without payment is comparable to an employee receiving an exorbitant salary for a minor chore that only deserves a minimal wage.

My reason for placing a great deal of emphasis on the point of earning rewards without effort or payment, is because there is a widespread acceptance that Divine blessing is not in the same category as, for example, the purchase of an expensive automobile or other material possession. The consciousness of payment is expected for material ownership or even for expensive services. The idea that material reward is only temporary is not placed within the concept of its payment.

Conversely, the *notion* that acquiring permanent relief, or achieving a degree of mastery over one's present and future course of events, does not require payment commensurate with the results, will inherently prevent the realization of these much sought after objectives. Our consciousness determines the outcome. Without a definitive awareness of the game plan, one is limited in the process of achieving a connection with the Tree of Life reality.

However, when a nonbeliever exercises skepticism solely on the premise that there is no record of such a phenomenon, or that he has never had that experience, this alone is not a valid reason for rejection. Every North American is familiar with the expression, "I'm from Missouri." It might aptly be translated as "Show me" or "I'll believe it only if I see it with my own two eyes."

Expressions such as these attest to the pride we place in our ability to "see the world as it really is." It implies that the person who is speaking is a "realist" who won't have the wool pulled over his eyes. In truth, Missouri would certainly be a sorry place if all the people there were to limit their comprehension of existence based solely on what they could see.

Words such as intuition, love, hope and faith would have to be removed from the dictionary. All religions would have to be abolished for, how many of us can attest to having truly seen the Lord? The point is, that our five senses are notorious for being bad judges of the world around us.

We all have, no doubt, been in a situation in which a sound is heard and every person in the room believes that sound came from a different place. The sense of taste can be easily fooled by chemical scents and additives. Taste, touch, smell, sight, hearing — all of our senses play tricks on us. Why then do we place so much faith in them? Where do we turn to find the truth?

Heisenberg's *Uncertainty Principle*[227] establishes an inherent, inextricable indeterminism in the web of our world. The physical world is, therefore, an illusion. The real world is one step beyond. Just because something is seen with the eyes does not mean that it exits any more than not seeing is proof that it does not exist. Through Kabbalah we peel away the layers of illusion so that we may connect to the Lightforce within. Clinging to accepted and programmed notions and ideas is, indeed, an impediment in achieving a higher awareness.

For a good starting point in our investigation into the essential idea of miracles let us now turn to the Zohar for some insights behind this paranormal phenomenon. We have succumbed, although incorrectly, to the computer which so visibly exposes the limitations of our human ability and understanding. The Zohar is the breath of fresh air necessary to revive us from our deep and long slumber.

Rabbi Abba then discoursed on the text: And the Lord spoke to the fish, and it vomited out Jonah upon the dry land.[228] "Where and when did the Lord speak to the fish?" he asked. "It was," he replied "at the time of Creation, when the Lord created the world, on the fifth day, when He created the fishes of the sea.[229] He then ordained and conditioned that a certain fish swallow up Jonah and retain him in its body three days and three nights and then eject him. And not only in this case, but with all that He had created did the Lord make certain stipulations."

Thus, on the first day, when He created the heavens, He required of them that they should take up Elijah into heaven by a whirlwind, and so it was, as it is written, "...and Elijah went up [and not the Lord *took* him up] by a whirlwind into heaven!"[230]

On the same day He created the Light and stipulated with it that the sun should become darkened in Egypt three days, as it is written, "And the Lord said unto Moses, bend your hand towards the heaven and there was a thick darkness in all the land of Egypt three days."[231]

On the second day He created the firmament to divide the waters from the waters, and in so doing He stipulated that they should separate between defilement and purity on behalf of Israel and be to them a means of cleansing, and so it was.

On the third day He made the dry land appear from the waters and caused the waters to be gathered together into one place, forming from them the sea.[232] He stipulated with it that it should allow the Israelites to pass through it on dry land and then overwhelm the Egyptians. And so it happened, as it is written, "...and the sea returned to its strength when the morning appeared"[233] where the term in the Bible *L'ethano* (to its strength), by a transposition of letters can be read *l'tano* (to its stipulation). In addition, the Lord stipulated with the earth that it should open its mouth on the occasion of the rebellion of Korah and swallow him up with all his company. And so it happened.[234]

On the fourth day[235], he created the sun and the moon, and He stipulated with the sun that it should stand still in the midst of heaven in the days of Joshua.[236] He also stipulated with the stars that they should wage war against Sisera.[237]

On the fifth day He created the fishes of the sea and the birds of heaven.[238] With the birds he stipulated that they should feed Elijah when he restrained the heaven from rain, as it is written: "And I have commanded the ravens to feed thee there!"[239] And He stipulated with the fishes of the sea to appoint one fish that should swallow up Jonah and then eject him.

On the sixth day He created Adam[240] and stipulated with him that a woman should descend from him who would sustain Elijah, as it is stated, "Behold I have commanded a widow there to sustain thee!"[241] Similarly, in regard to every unique phenomenon that has taken place in our world, the Lord had stipulated it from the time of Creation.

In the story of Jonah we have a representation of

the whole of a man's life-journey in this world. Jonah[242] boarding the ship is symbolic of man's soul that descends into this physical world to enter into his body. Why is she [the Soul] called Jonah (aggrieved)? Because as soon as she [the soul] becomes partner with the body in this world she [the soul] finds herself full of vexation and pain, as stated in Scriptures, one should not inflict pain upon his friend![243] Man, then journeys in this world as in a ship. The ship is sailing the great ocean which is likely to be torn apart, as stated, "so that the ship was likely to be broken."[244]

Furthermore, man in this world sins, imagining he can flee from the presence of his Master [fleeing from the universal law of action and reaction, cause and effect], who seems to take no notice or makes no appearance in our world. [Following on the heels of universal law], the Lord, [or producer of the universal scenario] then unleashes a furious tempest, for this is the decree of cause and effect judgment which constantly makes its appearance before the Lord and demands the effect (punishment) of man's action.

It is this judgment which assails the ship and calls to mind man's sins that it may pain him. Man is thus caught up by the tempest or stormy journey and is struck down with illness and misfortune, just as Jonah went down into the innermost part of the ship; and he lay, and was fast asleep.[245]

Although the man is prostrated, his soul does not

exert itself to return to the Lord in order to redeem his sins. And when it is stated the ship-master came to him, this is the good or positive inclination who is the general steersman, and said unto him, "how could you sleep at this time? Arise and call upon the Lord. Now is not the time for sleep, as they are about to take you to be tried for all you have done in this world. Repent of your sins!"[246]

Within this lengthy discourse of the Zohar, the idea and concepts of miracles are clearly set forth and how we achieve miracles in our daily activities. When the Zohar strikingly describes the six days of creation, the question of methodology must be raised. If it were the Lord's intent to perform those miracles some time in the future, why was it necessary that He make these stipulations at the time of creation? Certainly the Lord, the Omnipotent, could at his discretion perform these miracles whenever He felt the appropriate time for these miraculous events had come. In addition, does the Zoharic text imply that without this so called permission the sun, water, etc. could reject the request and stipulation of the Lord? If the Lord did not make the stipulation, does this indicate that somehow, somewhere, the Lord is powerless to impose His will over matters pertaining to the physical corporeal realm of reality, the Tree of Knowledge universe? Furthermore, what was the intent or energy-intelligent motivation that brought about the Lord's stipulations at the time of creation? Why did this point in time, at creation, take on such importance and significance?

However, on closer examination of the preceding Zohar, the revealment of its text leads us to a complete revision of our understanding concerning paranormal events. Whether they relate to global supernatural occurrences such as that which took place in Eastern Europe, or personal paranormal events, the Zohar provides a distinct clarification of miracles.

Addressing the question as to why the stipulations of the Lord were imposed at the time of creation, let us reflect upon another section of the Zohar[247] relating to the topic of Miracles.

> Rabbi Pinḥas was once going to see his daughter, the wife of Rabbi Shimon, who was ill. He was accompanied by the companions, and was riding on his donkey. [This is the illustrious donkey that lived during the era of Balaam some 1,400 years before].[248] On his way he met two Arabs, and said to them: "Has a voice ever been heard in this field?" They replied: "About former times we cannot say, but we know that in our own time there used to be robbers who waylaid men in this field. They once fell on some Jews with intent to cut them down, when there was heard from a distance in this field the voice of a donkey braying twice, and a flame of fire came into the field and burnt them, so that the Jews escaped." He said to them: "Arabs, Arabs, for the sake of this information that you have given me you shall be saved from other robbers who are lying in wait for you on the way."

> Rabbi Pinḥas wept, and said: Master of the Universe, you have caused this miracle to happen on my behalf, and those Jews were rescued and I did not know it. As stated in the Scriptures, "Give thanks to the Lord of lords, for His steadfast love endures forever. To Him who alone does great wonders, for His steadfast love endures forever!"[249]

How much kindness does the Lord do for men, and how many miracles does He cause to come about for them, and no one knows except Him!

A man may rise in the morning and a snake come to kill him, and he treads on the snake and kills it without knowing, but the Lord alone knows. A man goes on the road and robbers are in wait for him, and another comes and takes his place and he is saved, and does not know the kindness that the Lord has done with him or the miracle He has done on his behalf. The Lord alone does it and knows it.

He then said to the Companions: "Companions, what I really wanted to learn from the Arabs who frequent this field was whether they have heard the voice of the Companions who study the Torah, for Rabbi Shimon and Rabbi Elazar, his son and the rest of the Companions are in front of us without knowing of us. I was asking those Arabs about them, because I know that the voice of Rabbi Shimon shakes the field and the rocks. They have, however, told me something I did not know."

As they were going along, the Arabs returned to him and said: Old man, old man, you asked us concerning bygone days but not concerning this day in which we have seen wonder on wonder. We have seen five men sitting together and one old man among them. We saw the birds collecting and spreading their wings over his head, some going and others coming, so that there was always a shade over their heads. As the old man raised his voice, they were listening.

He said: that was what I wanted to know, Arabs, Arabs, may you have all the good fortune on this journey that you, desire. You have told me two things which have given me joy. They then proceeded on their way. Said the Companions to him: How are we to find the place where Rabbi Shimon is? He replied: Leave it to the Master (Lord) of the steps of my beast (donkey) who will guide its steps there. He then gave the rein to his donkey, which then turned off the road they were on and proceeded on the new path for two miles. The donkey began to bray three times. Rabbi Pinhas dismounted and said: Let us prepare ourselves to meet the presence of the *Atik Yomin*, the *Shekhinah* [the all embracing quantum consciousness] for now great faces and small faces [consciousness-students of Rabbi Shimon] will come out to us. Rabbi Shimon heard the braying of the donkey and said to the Companions: Let us rise for the voice of the donkey of the pious elder has aroused within us. Rabbi Shimon thereupon rose and his Companions also.

RABBI SHIMON CITED THE VERSE: "A PSALM. O SING UNTO THE LORD A NEW SONG, FOR HE HAS DONE MARVELOUS THINGS."[250]

The tonal accent on the word *mizmor* (psalm) here, he said, shows that this psalm has some special distinction. Who was it that uttered this song? It was the kine [cows] (that bore the Ark from the house of *Obed Edom*)[251] in their "moo-ing".... The word for "song" here is the masculine form *shir* whereas Moses designated his song by the feminine form, *Shirah*.[252] The reason is that in the time of Moses only the Ark itself was coming forth from captivity, but here the Ark was coming forth with what was deposited in it. "For he hath done marvelous things": this refers to what was done to the Philistines and their idols.

"His right hand hath wrought salvation for him,"[253] this means, for the psalm itself and the holy spirit concealed in it. [Meaning the *Shekhinah* which is also known by the code name "Song"and the Upper Holy Spirit known by its code name *Zeir Anpin*[254] is concealed within the *Shekhinah*. What is specifically meant by "His right hand?" This which the old man, the Patriarch Abraham who is right column, takes hold of within the "song," Psalm Ninety-Eight, and does not leave it in the hands of others. Now is the time to reveal a certain matter. As long as the right, *Ḥesed*, desires to perform a miracle, it takes hold of this "song" and gives it to Israel to make use of it].

Now if those kine [cows] for which miracles were an unusual thing, being vouchsafed to them only on that occasion, uttered this song in their mooing, how much more must we say that the braying of the donkey of the pious elder [Rabbi Pinḥas] signifies a song of praise! Do not think, Companions, that this has not been the manner of this donkey from the time the world was created. And if this was the case with the donkey of the wicked Balaam, how much more must it be so with the donkey of Rabbi Pinhas ben Yair.

Now is the time, Companions, to reveal something else. When the mouth of the donkey was created on the eve of Shabbat at twilight,[255] do you think that its mouth was open from that time, or that the Lord made stipulation with it from that time? Not so; there is here a mystery which has been transmitted to the wise who pay not heed to folly. The mouth of the donkey is the branch, degree and level of the original grade of that supernal one [since the origin of all physical entities originates from its metaphysical counterpart, i.e. there was *Adam Kadmon*,[256] the 99% metaphysical reality and then *Adam haRishon*[257] the physical appearance reality] which descended from the side of the females who reigned on the donkey and it [the metaphysical reality] spoke over and through it.

When the Lord created that supernal grade called the "mouth of the donkey" he enclosed it in the hollow of the great deep and kept it there till that day. When the time came He opened the hollow and it came forth and rested on the donkey and spoke.

So when it says that "the earth opened its mouth,"[258] [the additional word *Et,* the Hebrew word always refers to an additional concept within the verse] this relates to the Angel Dumah's intervention of the miraculous event.

"The mouth of the donkey"[259] [which verse contains the word *Et*] was controlled by the Angel Kadriel and the "mouth of the well"[260] was called Yahadriel.

These three "mouths" were created on the eve of the Shabbat. When the Lord sanctified the Shabbat, there arose a "mouth" superior and appointed over all other "mouths." Who is it? The day (Shabbat) which is called the "mouth of the Lord."[261]

A large mass of Zoharic text to digest at one time. I respectively urge the reader to review the two Zohar texts previously mentioned to assure a full comprehension of its profound insight into the mysteries and sometimes false myths concerning miracles.

Let us now return to the first Zohar mentioned where several questions were raised. Addressing the question as to why it was necessary for the Lord's stipulation to be made at the time of Creation: The first seven days of creation are considered the all-embracing, encompassing seed of creation. Of necessity, the seed must contain all the ultimate physical expression, from root to the ultimate and final destination, which is the fruit. At the seed level the varied potential tracks all exist as one unified central force, part of the all-embracing unity concept. Why this fundamental picture of reality escapes the wisdom of the scientist is more of a mystery than the mystery of humanity itself.

The parallel tracks that exist in our universe, depending upon which of them is *taken*, will determine the ultimate outcome for the individual.[262]

Just as the leaf of a maple tree cannot suddenly decide

one day to become the leaf of an aspen, or an apple tree to become an orange tree, man too must exist within the context of certain predestined genetic and cultural parameters. Only after various conditions are met (moisture, soil, sunlight) can the chain of events begin which will allow the undifferentiated elements within the seed to express themselves as separate entities.

Consequently, changes of any kind must inherently take place at the seed level. Subsequently, if a possibility for altering any future developments were to emerge, this ability must have already existed at the seed level. Therefore, the conditions and stipulations stated in the Zohar were set down and included within the seed of Creation.

What exactly did the Lord have in *mind* with these stipulations? But then again, what are we referring to when we speak of the "Mind of the Lord." By means of Kabbalah we can truly see into the mind of the Lord. When science attempts to answer the really deep issues, such as the origin and meaning of the universe, there is a tendency to retreat into the immaterial reality.

Science normally takes for granted that the natural laws of our universe can be revealed by human intellect. Yet, so much remains a deep mystery. The Kabbalistic explanation for this startling mystery is that the total unfolding of our universe must come in stages. The sole reason for the scientific discoveries in the twentieth century that shook the very foundation of 300 years of scientific principles was that Rabbi Ashlag revealed the Kabbalistic Theory of Rabbi Isaac Luria.

The sudden appearance of the relativity and quantum theories that emerged through scientists like Einstein and Bohr occurred because the time for these revelations had come. One of the most curious ideas set forth by quantum physics is that the separateness that we attribute to everything from tables and man on down to subatomic particles might just be a human illusion.

Danish physicist Neils Bohr originally proposed this theory when he noticed that two particles emitted from a decaying particle will have the same spatial accommodation to the site of emission. Suppose someone placed a firecracker in an apple, with the explosion causing the apple to split in half, the two halves will move away in opposite, yet parallel, directions. He also proved, on a subatomic level, that if the path of one of these particles is changed, there will be an equal effect on the other particle, simultaneously. Einstein noted that this fact implied a *level of organization* that we have yet to comprehend.

David Bohm, English physicist, also agreed to a more *subtle* level of organization than we can presently observe: The idea that at a certain level separate entities are actually part of the same one something. What is missing from quantum physics concerning *reality* is an understanding of what this "whole unified reality" consists.

The Kabbalistic parallel universe idea of the Tree of Life and Tree of Knowledge realities mentioned elsewhere in this volume is exactly what scientists need to know about our universe. Then, their dilemma of the mind of the Lord would no longer remain a mystery.

The thought behind the Creation, is to share with mankind.[263] We are taught by the Kabbalist the simple fundamental idea that by the Lord's thought alone, everything was created and immediately brought to its completion. This principle also applies to the thought of man. A large number of thoughts may go into the manifestation of any thought. However, preceding all these, already in the very first thought of the act is present its final conclusion.

For example, in planning a new home, the first thought is the picture of the complete structure, or how the home will look. Before its final conclusion, however, many details have to be worked out and acted upon. The completed home follows only after many diversified thoughts and actions. However, the final result was already present in the initial thought.

The multifaceted thoughts and observations are noticeable only at the Tree of Knowledge level of reality. At this illusionary level of reality, things seem to have separateness and consequently diversity such as good and evil. At the Tree of Life reality level separateness simply does not exist. Our naked eye and rational intelligence of four to six percent obviously cannot serve as interference patterns for visualizing this reality.

The Tree of Knowledge reality is almost like the situation in the tale of the blind men and the elephant. One feels the leg and thinks it's a tree. The other feels the trunk and thinks it's a snake. Neither of them sees the whole elephant. Once we access into the Tree of Life reality, this permits us to see the quantum level of the elephant, or the whole.

Kabbalistic prayer offers a mechanism whereby we can potentially hook into the whole image, although we may never, in our physical corporeal body, understand the existence of the *Shekhinah*, the collective unconscious.

However, we can tap into the *Shekhinah* collective consciousness despite the personal experience and memories that threaten to inhibit our connection to unlimited consciousness. A bricklayer, for example may assume that he could not possibly understand psychiatry. An airplane manufacturer would dismiss the idea that he could engage in medical practice when his experience or education did not incorporate medical knowledge.

This is what the Kabbalist refers to as the separateness and division that is governed by the Tree of Knowledge reality of good and evil. On the surface in everyday life, things often appear to be without arrangement or form. However, on closer examination, there seems to be a hidden order. Let us take for example, Morse Code messages. To one unfamiliar with the Morse Code, it is a seemingly random jumble of sounds, but to the initiate, the Code is an intelligent signal.

Were it not for Kabbalistic knowledge, the future ecology of our civilization might well remain in jeopardy, and the end of the earth might be a foreseeable reality. The oft quoted Zohar,[264] "Woe unto those who will live at that time [Age of Aquarius], yet happy those who will live at that time," attests to the fact of a dual cosmic reality. Thus, there appears to exist a cosmos within a cosmos.

The stipulations mentioned previously, are the Zoharic contention that within each day of Creation, side by side with the possible evolution of the Tree of Knowledge reality, there was an accompanying reality, the Tree of Life universe, where once accessed, the normal events of chaos brought about by the Creation of the Tree of Knowledge reality came to an abrupt halt. This was evidenced by the splitting of the Red Sea. Control over the physical, illusionary reality came about by Moses tapping and accessing into the Tree of Life reality.[265]

In actuality, the Hebrew word for "miracle", *Nes,* has over the millennium become corrupted and misinterpreted. Exploring the origin of this word *Nes,* we find its translation referring to another idea, apparently having no connection with the idea of "miracle."

In the following verse the word *Nes* takes on an entirely different meaning:

> When the Ark went forth, Moses said, "Arise, O Lord, and scatter your enemies! Let your foes *flee*, (*yanusu*) before you."[266]

Another striking example of the true and accurate definition of the word *Nes* comes from the Red Sea splitting event where the Egyptians gave chase and approached the Israelites at the Red Sea. The chariots became bogged down, and they could move only with great difficulty. The Egyptians cried out,

> "Let us flee (*anusa*) from Israel. The Lord is fighting for them against Egypt."[267]

In the previous two verses mentioned, the word *Nes* unquestionably refers to an act of flight or fleeing. How can we possibly reconcile the idea of miracles with the notion of fleeing? To make matters even worse, and add some greater confusion, the Biblical word for miracle is addressed by another word entirely, *mofeth*. "... when a prophet or a person who has visions in a dream arises among you. He may present you with a sign or miracle (*mofeth*), and on the basis of that sign or miracle (*mofeth*) say to you, let us try out a different god. "[268]

To unscramble the mystery and dilemma we turn to another mystifying section of the Bible.[269] In a battle between Israel and Amalek in Rephidim Moses told Joshua to choose men, and to prepare for battle while he was to stand on top of a hill with the staff of the Lord in his hand. Moses, Aaron, and Hur went to the top of the hill.

And it came to pass, when Moses held up his
hand, that Israel prevailed: and when he let down
his hand, Amalek prevailed. But Moses' hands
were weary; and they took a stone and put it
under him and he sat on it; and Aaron and Hur
supported his hands, one on each side, and his
hands were steady until sunset. And Joshua was
able to break the ranks of Amalek and his allies
with the sword.

Indeed a strange manner of waging war. If the raising of
the hands of Moses was sufficient to create victory, what was the
purpose in having Joshua wage war? Why did the raising or lowering of Moses' hands result in Israel winning or losing the battle?
How did Aaron and Hur contribute to the war scenario?

Even more confusing are the final three verses:

The Lord said to Moses, "Write this as a reminder
in the book and repeat it carefully to Joshua. I
will totally obliterate the memory of Amalek from
under the heavens. And Moses built an altar and
he called it "The Lord is my *Nes*" (miracle or
fleeing). The Lord is on the Lord's throne. The
Lord shall be at war with Amalek for all generations.

If the idea stated here is that the Lord will wage war, then
why all the fuss with Joshua, Aaron, Hur and Moses?
Furthermore, the final verse seems to indicate an ongoing battle
with Amalek, when in reality it was stated earlier that Joshua
broke the ranks of Amalek with the sword. In addition, what, if
any, is the deeper significance relating to the raising and lowering
of the arms of Moses? If this event implies Divine meditation —

the lowering is the cessation, the raising is the activation of Divine intervention — why does the event become expressed the way it is stated in Scriptures?

The Kabbalist always guards against literal interpretations of ancient texts, and is especially watchful when interpreting Biblical writings. This is not to suggest that a literal interpretation of the Bible does not make good reading. It does. And, indeed, it cannot be denied that the Bible provides a most valuable historical record. Rather, the reason the Kabbalist probes beneath the surface of Biblical interpretation is the unshakable conviction that the real meaning of the Bible is not to be found in the "outer garments," the tales, stories and narrations. The meaning of the Bible, like the Light, must remain concealed.

The Bible, according to Kabbalistic wisdom, is a cosmic code, which must be deciphered. Every word, line, and passage harbors a sublime hidden meaning. Thus, to lift from the Bible certain passages concerning miracles and interpret them literally is, in the Kabbalist's view, to engage in an exercise in futility.[270]

Consequently, for the Kabbalist, the superficial relationship that appears between the war waged by the Lord and that of Moses does not reveal the essence of the meaning concerning Amalek. Let us, therefore, explore the Zohar for an in-depth clarification of this complex Biblical narration. Why did Moses abstain from fighting the first battle which the Lord Himself mandated? Because he was able to divine the true meaning of his Master's command. Hence he said: "I will prepare myself for the war above and you, Joshua, prepare yourself for the war below." This is the meaning of the words: "When Moses lifted up his hand, Israel prevailed,"[271] namely Israel above. Therefore, Moses did not participate in the war on earth, so that he might throw himself with greater zeal into the real war which is in Heaven or the Upper Realm and thus promote victory on earth.

> Said Rabbi Shimon: Let us not think lightly of
> this war with Amalek. Verily, from the creation of
> the world until then [Exodus], and since then till
> the coming of Messiah, there has been and will be
> no war like that, nor can even the war
> Armageddon be compared with it. This, not
> because of the mighty armies taking part in it, but
> because it was launched against all that the Lord,
> [the Lightforce] represents.[272]

What seems to emerge from the Zohar is that action of
any sort originates in the upper or metaphysical realm. This can
be seen in the activities of humankind. There is no doubt that
prior mental thought precedes action. The metaphysical realm
must, of necessity, come before the human body takes any
action.

The metaphysical is always regarded as the primary reality; its ultimate manifestation is a web of material, physical patterns. To say it in another way, the manifestation of thought precedes the emergence of material patterns. The world must be
viewed as a complicated web of infinite events, material and non-
material, that determine the tissue of the whole. Then, and only
then, can we understand the dynamic interplay of our cosmos.

In the Kabbalistic world view of cosmic reality, the con-
ceptual tissue of war is not fought at this level of ours. Take for
example the Second World War. Before the physical devastation
attributed to war took place on our physical, terrestrial level, the
scenario had already taken place long before within the upper,
metaphysical realm. The true course of war is the activity manifested by mankind. The battleground is the metaphysical realm.

The players are the forces of the Dark Lord, as opposed to the positive activities of mankind which bring support and assistance to the Lightforce.

The holocaust and devastation of fifty million human lives during World War Two were already ordained by the magnitude of the negative activity of mankind. This expression supported the Dark Lord in his function of bringing chaos and disorder to our physical world. What humankind experienced between the years of 1939-1945 was merely a physical replay of a battle which had taken place before its physical expression was witnessed by mankind.

This is similar to viewing, at the present time, a film which had been taken during the war some 50 years earlier. The action is very real. However, the war had been waged long before. So too must we elevate our awareness to the fact that what is experienced at our physical level, is a scenario that already took place and the players in the film and its outcome depend on the human activity, positive or negative, of prior days or lifetimes.

The significance that seems to emerge from the Zohar is the need to establish within ourselves the Kabbalistic understanding of cause and effect. The Zohar recognizes the futility of linking *local* cause with effect. Only that which apparently connects a seen cause to an observable effect is assumed by scientists to fall within the category of linking cause with effect.

The Quantum Theory substantiated the 2,000 year Zoharic perspective that a man's actions, even though they may be separated from their effects by time, space and motion, are not lost or forgotten. The acts of the characters in the Zoharic *Amalek* narration demonstrated what was necessary to change or alter outcomes of future events, and even our individual destinies.

When Moses raised his hands, this action was a definitive clue to what was required when connection to the Tree of Life reality is to be established. One must *flee* or *leave* the realm of the Tree of Knowledge illusionary reality, where chaos and disorder reign supreme. The altruistic characters in the Zoharic narration demonstrated their empathy, sensitivity and understanding. Their positive consciousness and kind deeds symbolized their connection with the Tree of Life reality.

Moses, Aaron and Hur portrayed the very essence of self sacrifice, a determination to resemble the sharing attributes of the Lightforce. Their communion with the Tree of Life was irrevocable. Thus, whatever fate might have been in store for these individuals was transformed into what we refer to as *miracles*, or the continuity and certainty that belongs to the world of Tree of Life.

They represented the three column system[273] so necessary in man's attempt to reach the Lightforce, the only hope for mankind's future. Positive action was, and is, the necessary ingredient in reversing mankind's struggle within the Tree of Knowledge reality. Tolerance for our fellow man was, and can be the turning point towards altering humankind's history of suffering, war and bloodshed.

A Lightforce consciousness and awareness can bring us to the ultimate realization that intolerance, revenge and devastation have never, nor will ever bring about the final solution of certainty and self-fulfillment. The dreams of mankind will *never* be achieved at the expense of others, no matter how noble the cause.

The Kabbalist steers clear of the realm of the physical illusion of uncertainty, the underlying reason for man's intolerance. Why in the world would mankind find it necessary to wage war, even in the name of the Lord, or for any other "justifiable" reason, when tomorrow and forever brings with it the assurance of the Lightforce that we need not suffer the traumas that usually accompany the lifestyle misery of chaos? The short-lived satisfaction of revenge cannot erase the tears of a parent when a child becomes a victim of universal slaughter.

The physical realm that seldom provides us with miracles is the realm of uncertainty. Perhaps we will be "lucky"; perhaps "unlucky." The Tree of Knowledge reality is the domain of those who abandon themselves to the Desire to Receive for the Self Alone. Greed raises its ugly head only when there is fear for whatever tomorrow may bring, namely uncertainty. And when one chooses uncertainty, the illusionary Tree of Knowledge of chaos and disorder, we find ourselves raising the question "why me?", as misfortune suddenly takes control of our lives.

In fact, bad things happen only to those who are trapped in uncertainty, the illusionary reality. Had more people been exposed to Kabbalistic concepts and the reasons behind them, less emphasis would be placed on material values, which come and go with the "uncertainty principle." In no way is this meant to be a negation of the physical reality, which is of vital importance to the soul's cycle of correction. However, we should always remember and temper our physical actions with the knowledge that it is certainty, the Tree of Life reality, that provides the uninterrupted flow of certainty and fulfillment, the miracles that we so often hope for.

Consequently, we now can understand the deeper significance of *Amalek* and the continuous war against it. *Amalek* has the same numerical value as the Hebrew word for uncertainty, *safek*, two hundred and forty. The Biblical text is not referring to the physical game of warfare between the Israelites and a nation called *Amalek*.

This text relates to the ongoing struggle between mankind and the Dark Lord of uncertainty, the nemesis wreaking havoc on universal man. Without dominion over the Dark Lord of uncertainty that is the desire to receive for the self alone, one cannot perceive the higher realms of the cosmos. We must achieve a mastery of the cosmic level of certainty and gain access to where past, present, and future are one.

The three characters of the *Amalek* scenario merely provide us with the methodology by which miracles become a daily occurrence. The *Nes* (miracle) no longer depends on being *lucky* or *unlucky*. Therefore the text states "And Moses built an altar and named it *Ad'nai Nissi*."[274] By virtue of the use of the exalted Name *Ad'nai* (The Tetragrammaton) does one achieve *Nissi*, "my flight" from the uncertainty level of reality to the realm of the certainty level of the Tree of Life.

Regarding the verse "and Moses said to Joshua," asks the Zohar:[275]

Why to him, who was then but a "youth?"[276] Were there in Israel no greater warriors then Joshua? The reason was that Moses in his wisdom was aware that it was not going to be merely a battle against flesh and blood, but against the negative angelic force of Samael, who was coming down to assist *Amalek*.

Now Joshua, "the youth" had reached at that time a high degree of spiritual perception. Not as high as Moses, who was united with the *Shekhinah*, but his soul was, in fact, attached to the supernal region called "youth," the Metatron Angel. Now when Moses perceived that *Samael* was going to fight for *Amalek*, he thought: "this young man, Joshua, will surely stand against him and prevail!"

Therefore, he said to him: "go out and fight against *Amalek*! It is your battle, the battle here below, and I will prepare myself for the battle above. Choose, therefore, worthy men, righteous and the sons of the righteous, to accompany you."

Said Rabbi Shimon: at the moment when Joshua, "the young man" began to fight *Amalek* the "young man" above was stirred, and was equipped with weapons prepared by his "Mother," the *Shekhinah*, for the battle in order to avenge the covenant with the "sword." Moses equipped himself for the war above. "His hands were heavy"[277] meaning honorable, holy hands that had never been defiled, hands worthy to wage the war above.

"And Aaron and Ḥur kept up his hands, the one on one side, and the other on the other side, and his hands were steady." This cannot be taken in the literal sense; what it means is that Aaron represented his "side," (the right column of Mercy) and Ḥur his "side" (the left column of Judgment). And Moses' hands between the two represented the central column.

The Zohar is strikingly clear when it proposes for mankind the tools by which we can connect with the realm of certainty which is the essential meaning of this event as decoded by the Zohar. Miracles are not in any way related to an idea of being lucky or unlucky. The important lesson taught within the Biblical text is that the text cannot, nor should it be interpreted in the ordinary sense of its translation. The inner meaning as understood by the Zohar is the only reliable and truthful meaning of the Biblical intent.

Furthermore, we are powerless within the physical, corporeal level of existence to maintain a balanced level of certainty. The Biblical text concerning the Tree of Knowledge so stated when it referred to the Tree of Knowledge as Good and Evil. There exists within this realm the illusion of good, only to disappear when evil or misfortune overruns and overtakes our lives. Fortunes come and go. Health is steady only until the next illness is upon us, peace be with us.

Hope and prayer are simply not the tools that we can rely upon unless we make use of the Kabbalistic method of quantum prayer. The two thousand years of chaos and order readily attest to this futility. Only with a proper consciousness, attitude and the tools of Kabbalistic prayer can we hope to achieve a communion with the Tree of Life reality.

Then, and only then, does the Lightforce become revealed, and then certainty no longer becomes an elusive concept so often absent from our life journey. When we have achieved an elevated state of consciousness and awareness, we begin to realize that it is not our ability, brain or aggressiveness that is the decisive factor in our good fortune. The Lightforce does all the planning, motivation and infusion of our state of consciousness that permits certainty and good fortune to become our journey's trademark.

This, then, provides the reader with a full and clear explanation of the previously mentioned lengthy Zohar concerning the donkeys of Balaam and Rabbi Pinḥas ben Yair.

Another discussion relating to the code concept of "donkey" is found in the following Zohar:

> Said the Companions to him: "How are we to find the place where Rabbi Shimon is?" He replied: "Leave it to the Master (Lord) of the steps of my beast who will guide its steps there." He then gave the rein to his donkey.[278]

What emerges from the preceding Zohar is that the uniqueness of these donkeys was, in the words of the Zohar, "the Master (Lord) of the steps will guide its steps." In other words we, for the most part, observe separateness in the five senses. On the other hand, these donkeys were created at the time of creation within the unified concept of the all embracing whole, the Lightforce.

At the terrestrial level of existence, the donkeys performed as a computerized mechanism. In the same way, most people behave according to their computerized cassette of a prior lifetime.[279] People differ from animals to the extent that man must strive for and achieve a communion with the celestial realm of the Tree of Life. However, by stipulation at Creation the separateness we as humans experience did not apply to these donkeys.

All animals, vegetables, and inanimate entities are positioned from the very beginning of their existence to follow a prescribed set of cassettes. They do not, nor can they, deviate from these natural universal laws and principles. Only mankind enjoys the possibility of free will. Having free will mankind may prefer to join forces with the Dark Lord and uncertainty. However, that may not be as enjoyable.

Stipulations mentioned in the Zohar allude to a direct intervention by the Lightforce into the realm of the Tree of Knowledge reality. If, indeed, the illusionary Tree of Knowledge reality reigned supreme in our world of existence, we could never survive its impact. The uncertainty, the ups and downs, would prevail more often than not.

For this reason, the Lord injected these *stipulations* as a control device that placed restrictions on the Dark Lord and his fleet. Without these limitations even the few years of respite between world wars and financial stability would remain a dream. The singular reason for the little that we do experience from time to time is the Dark Lord's[280] bait and inducement thrown at us. The Dark Lord's objective is to lure us into a smug feeling that we are in control of our lives.

When we are healthy, successful in business, or have wonderful relationships, the Dark Lord induces us to believe that it is our brain, our efforts that brought about the satisfaction we enjoy. We and our egotistic feelings (the Dark Lord's major weapon) are responsible for our success. We are indeed in control.

However, once we reach this plateau and the Dark Lord is convinced that his trap has been triumphantly secured, he drops us like a hot potato. He removes the contentment by abandoning the aspect of "good"[281] in the Tree of Knowledge reality, and suddenly chaos and misfortune reign supreme; strengthening our egos to the point that we recognize our stupid mistakes, and yet, retain the ego that we are still brilliant.

And so the battle rages on and on. In any dispute, each side becomes convinced that his or her cause is a cause for justice. Now, who determines what is to be considered justifiable and which principles are to be eliminated? The decision is usually based upon our own conclusions, forever thinking with our minds and egos. Each individual knows best, except when failure appears. Did we pause for a moment and reflect on what basis we have validated our conclusions? This is precisely the cunning device used by the Dark Lord. Throw us a bone or a scrap of illusionary contentment sufficient to establish in our mind and ego that we are in control of our daily affairs.

And when chaos becomes the rule of everyday existence, our ego has already been developed to the point where we either blame others for our misfortune or think back how this difficult situation might, perhaps, have been avoided. The Dark Lord revels in merriment. He has infused the satanic venom of illusionary control, egocentricity, into the essential vein of his intended victim. Once his lethal dose has been administered, he leaves the scene of the deathless crime and moves on to other pastures.

The Dark Lord's victim now seeks the illusionary options of revenge as the case may be, or blames it on the Lord, for abandoning him or her in a time of need. The Dark Lord is the culprit behind every case of misfortune. He has so hoodwinked mankind that, for the most part, few of us are prepared to accept the fact that we are responsible for the disorder in our lives.

However, if we can follow the teachings of the previous Zohar, then we come to the realization that good-fortune can never become a permanent experience unless we rise to an alternate level of consciousness. This means that we arrive at the sensible conclusion that we alone can never achieve control over our lives without communion with the Lightforce.

Once we achieve a connection with the Lightforce, then the all-knowing, all-embracing unity becomes an active participator in our daily activities. Not limited or confined to the obstruction and interruption of time, space and motion, where the past, present and future all exist as a unified concept, the Lightforce then motivates and initiates activities, as well as so-called miracles, in our daily lives.

Inasmuch as the essential characteristic of the Lightforce is one of sharing its beneficence, the Dark Lord cannot create a beachhead for chaos and disorder to place its stamp on our lives. When we come to the realization that only the Lightforce can provide continuous health, good relationships, and financial success, then we have, in fact, prevented the brain and ego from drawing the venom of the Dark Lord. This matter is as simple as striking a match in a dark room, where no effort is necessary to remove the darkness.

This is what Rabbi Pinḥas meant when he remarked, "How much kindness does the Lord do for men, and how many miracles does He cause to come about for them, and no one knows except Him." Once we connect to the Lightforce, we are no longer governed by the traumas of each day. We exist in a realm where time no longer is a constant. For those connected, the stipulations inserted at the time of Creation exist for us today and everyday. Yesterday and tomorrow are only an illusion of time as we know it.

However, I repeat again, our consciousness must be at a level where we have come to the essential truth that: I am not in control, unless I permit the Lightforce to act on my behalf. My ego does not interfere with the quantum consciousness of the Lightforce. I am perfectly convinced that the Lightforce can only impart its beneficence of certainty. When discomfort or other forms of stress make their appearance, I know these are only a test to ascertain whether I still know the Lightforce is with me at all times. At that moment of testing, the Dark Lord will make every effort to inject an uncertainty consciousness. However, the moment I recognize the uncomfortable situation as being one of illusionary nature, this too shall pass, for the end result of the particular activity must reach its final destination of contentment and fulfillment.

To achieve this level of consciousness we must be prepared to exert effort of some sort. We cannot play our little games with the Lightforce. Whenever we decide it is "I" in control, then the Lightforce will take a backseat and permit our egos to take over the task of achieving our objectives. We must surely remember the Kabbalistic doctrine of "no coercion in spirituality." The Lightforce will only intervene when we acknowledge that only the Lightforce is in control of our lives.

Another requirement is the quantum connection to the Lightforce. Our thoughts and objectives cannot be one of a restrictive or limited nature. The Lightforce contains the entire quantum of beneficence. Limiting our objectives cannot be reconciled with the quantum and unlimited ability of the Lightforce to share its limitless beneficence.

Consequently, in our prior discussion concerning the uniqueness of Kabbalistic prayer, we now have arrived at an understanding why only through quantum prayer do we have the ability to communicate with the Lord. The Lord's nature is one of quantum. A prayer that includes anything less than a quantum capacity can never draw the Lightforce of the Lord into our daily lives. The Lightforce must serve and share its certainty through channels of a quantum quality.

This then is the Kabbalistic interpretation of *Nes*, miracles. We must flee from the Tree of Knowledge reality of limitation and uncertainty. Then, and only then, is certainty demonstrated in our lives. Otherwise known as miracles they become operative in our lives. We must flee from our ego which places limitations and the illusionary idea that we are in control.

This is the paradoxical nature of miracles. When I dismiss any notion of control, I then gain access to the true reality of Lightforce control. When I believe that "I" have control over the affairs that influence my life, then I must suffer the consequences of uncertainty, lack of control over matters pertaining to my life.

With all of the aforementioned concepts now revealed by the Zohar, we can at this time return to the event of the Splitting of the Red Sea and the many questions that were raised in this connection. But first let us remember that the Lightforce of the Lord simply does not choose the persons It will or will not grace with Its beneficence and shower them with miracles.

This notion is so ingrained in the minds of people of all religious persuasions. When matters suddenly turn around for the better, their response then is, "the Lord has answered our prayers." This attitude thus leaves us with the impression that when things go belly up or become worse, we can attribute the lack of response or lack of improvement to the insensitivity of the Lord or simply, "the Lord refuses to respond to my prayers."

"Where were you, Lord, when I needed you most?" is the feeling of anguish and sorrow for most of mankind. The track record, trademark of civilization certainly indicates a lack of communication between ourselves and the Lord. What went wrong in a situation such as this?

The Kabbalistic viewpoint regarding this matter is quite clear and definitive. This never was nor will ever be the abandonment of the Lord toward his creation or created beings. Mankind brings upon itself the consequences of its positive or negative actions. Nonetheless, the Bible, decoded, takes us one step further. In the event we were inclined towards negative activity we still are given the opportunity to turn any situation around.

The underlying reason for chaos and misfortune is the lack of useful tools to create a communion between ourselves and the Lord. Even in a situation where we are suddenly confronted by a condition of chaos, and our intentions have in the past been positive, then our problem is not one of a Lord who is not listening to our prayers. Rather, we do not possess the information or channels to draw down into our lives the Lightforce and Its beneficence. The Lightforce desires to share Its beneficence even more than the individual desires to receive it.

There should never exist within our lives a thought of "why do bad things happen to good people?" I am not suggesting that when we are faced with misfortune we must accept it as an action of the Lord. The natural laws and principles of this universe are known to all of us. One of the essential rules is "ignorance of the law is no excuse."

When the Zohar opens for us a new world of awareness, its fundamental purpose is to raise our consciousness to ask questions never raised before. And more importantly we must always place the word "why" up front to any and all information thrown at us. So long as we do not have an appropriate answer to the "whys" raised, our information is either lacking or wrong.

Kabbalah provides us with the only complete system toward improving our well-being. No further research programs are required. The final results are all in. What remains is for us to remove the blinders placed upon mankind by the forces of the Dark Lord. We must not permit our consciousness to accept any chaotic circumstances nor to settle for less than our needs in the absence of normal solutions.

Never forget, my dear reader, the declaration of the Zohar[282] referring to the Age of Aquarius:

> In the days of Messiah there will no longer be the necessity for one to request of his neighbor "teach me wisdom," as it is written, "one day they will no longer teach every man his neighbor and every man his brother, saying know the Lord. For they shall *all know* Me, from the youngest to the oldest of them."[283]

The Zohar here expresses the idea that the Messianic era will usher in a period of unprecedented enlightenment. Messianism, representing the essence of hope and optimism, is bound up with, and dependent upon, true knowledge, the sublime wisdom of the Kabbalah. With worldwide dissemination of the Zohar expanding at an ever increasing rate, the fulfillment of Jeremiah's prophecy, "they shall all *know*" is closer to reality than ever before in history.

To confuse the issue further, the famous 20th century Danish physicist Neils Bohr said, "If you don't see it, it just isn't there." But surely the world out there exists whether or not we are looking at it. The chair upon which I am sitting may have disappeared, subatomically, but I am not likely to fall to the floor.

The answer lies in the consciousness of the mind. The mind element appears to be essential to our observation of the real world. What the scientists are saying, without knowing what they are really implying, is the Zoharic concept of "stipulation" that has been discussed in this chapter. In other words, because we have decided that we are seated on a chair, the physical chair responds to *our* consciousness that a chair exists.

However, touching upon a more serious note, we may and should ask of ourselves, if the physicists — Neils Bohr and his colleagues — are indeed correct in their conclusions concerning reality, then why can't a person with cancer send signals along nerves to enhance defenses and make the body fight more aggressively against disease? Why can't the patient deal with illness the way the physicists deal with an object like a chair? "If you don't observe it, it isn't there."

To complicate matters even further, Werner Heisenberg, the world-acclaimed German physicist and Nobel Laureate, introduced the dilemma of his "uncertainty principle." Simply stated, the premise of this principle is that we can *never* trust our senses completely and probably what we see is a questionable reality. Coupled with this fact that we have no certainty in this world is our arch enemy, the Dark Lord. In the interim, the Dark Lord is out there convincing us how brilliant and understanding we really are. He does not permit our egos to falter, nor does he permit us to develop a higher awareness in order to prevent us from escaping his grip upon mankind.

It is, therefore, intriguing and most ironic that we fail to adopt the Kabbalistic approach to logic by asking "why?" We continue to use outmoded logic and procedures. We seem to prefer the instant, temporary solution rather than researching the origin, the Kabbalah. The reason why the "uncertainty principle" has not received full recognition by the layman is due in great measure to the inadequate understanding of the principle by the scientist. The problems that the principles themselves raise are beyond what the present day scientist can deal with.

The "brain trusts" and "think tanks" of today admit they are unable to solve the world's most urgent problem. A complete understanding of the "uncertainty principle" will bring about a major shift in human behavior. Before embarking on any ambitious plans of negative activity, when convinced of uncertainty, a pause will become the order of the day.

As previously stated, the uncertainty principle is similar to the illusionary realm of the Tree of Knowledge. The layman, who for centuries had been shut-off from information reserved for a few knowledgeable physicists will easily access into the reservoir of quantum consciousness in this Messianic era. The doubts and uncertainties that scientists are beset with, will not in any way affect the ordinary individual.

Bohr and Heisenberg now substantiate the claim of the two thousand-year-old Zohar that mankind exists in the realm of illusion, and in the same breath declare that our consciousness supersedes all material and corporeal entities. Then why can't we remove the physical chaos all around us? A problem that science cannot deal with.

However, the Zohar makes it quite clear that there does exist a realm known as the Tree of Life reality. Once mankind becomes consciously connected with this reality the various situations such as cancer, financial upheaval and distressing relationships cease to exist. The Kabbalist, like the quantum physicist, understands that human consciousness has the unique ability to influence and even radically alter the physical nature of the universe.

The realization and successful implementation of this phenomenon can be achieved by connecting with the Tree of Life reality and the Lightforce. These famous scientists were actually saying what is said in the Bible: there are two states of existence. The scientists were revealing the illusionary, uncertainty nature of our physical reality. The Zohar two thousand years earlier related this physical reality to the Tree of Knowledge existence of reality. However, problems related to this uncertainty were the extensions of their theories, namely, why can't we control physical diseases with our consciousness?

The dilemma facing the scientists today in this Age of Aquarius is the dichotomy between the theoretical and the manifest states of reality. When Einstein returned from the classroom without the key to his apartment, he still could not walk through the front door, notwithstanding his conclusion that the door is an illusion. He was not capable of determining which stock investment would move upwards tomorrow despite his Relativity Theory that established the principle that the past, present and future are all in the "here and now."

When a scientist begins talking about an elastic time that can be extended or reduced, stretched or shrunk, places where time no longer exists as we know it, established laws of science must be reconsidered. Though such forms of time may appear to be acceptable to most of us, it nevertheless opens the door to even more and stranger phenomena. It seems to challenge our most rigid laws and principles of logic.

The scientific theory of time relates to the concept advanced by the Tree of Life reality. If we are deeply connected with the Lightforce, then material chaos like cancer no longer exists. If the front door represents a limitation, then, indeed, the door ceases to exist. However, as I mentioned previously, there are two requirements. One stipulates the significance of our consciousness. No change in our observation of reality can ever take place unless our consciousness undergoes an altered state. I refer to an acceptance of the illusionary frame of all material corporeal matter.

Eugene Wigner, Nobel prize winner in physics, *believes* that consciousness itself *alters* the world itself because it alters the observation of the subject matter, as in the case of the "disappearing" chair. The now I see you, now I don't, kind of idea. What he implied is that we experience the world the way we do only because we choose to experience it that way. Unfortunately, had Wigner been more in tune with the Kabbalistic perspective of reality, he would have understood that we possess very little free will in how we observe and appraise future events.

The essential problem facing Wigner and all other famous scientists is that they are not certain as to what this "thing" called consciousness is. The four or five-percent consciousness is an automatic feature of the physical brain.[284] The mind is merely the channel by which we connect to the varied levels of consciousness which belong to the upper realm of the cosmos. From a Kabbalistic perspective, there is no hidden power within our subconscious mind.

The infinite intelligence of the cosmos, the Lightforce, can reveal anything and everything we need to know at any moment in time, provided we are *open-minded* and receptive. Once we alter our consciousness from a Tree of Knowledge reality and accept this level of reality as illusionary, then we have opened the channels of the mind to tap the awesome power and knowledge of the Lightforce within the Tree of Life reality. Though invisible, its forces are powerful.

While we remain oblivious to the future, maintaining the communion with the Lightforce, the Lightforce directs the future events in a certainty journey of good health, financial success and improvement in our relationships. Consequently, the Kabbalah completely disagrees with the scientific premise mentioned before that "consciousness alters the observation of the world." We do not intervene or change past, present or future.

Our free will consists solely of the choice between the Tree of Life reality and the parallel universe of the Tree of Knowledge illusionary level, the trademark of which is chaos and uncertainty. The future, not the present, can be altered by our consciousness. Rather, all possible futures happen precisely in accordance with the cassette of prior lifetimes. They are programmed by cosmic computerized printouts.[285]

Essentially, there is no free will as proposed by the quantum theory. However, we do have a degree of freedom that is almost limitless. We *can* and should determine how the *Tikune* process evolves within our present lifetime. We can move and spring from universe to universe whenever we so choose. However, we must always remember the requirements which will make possible this novel space journey towards the true reality of continuous joy, a beneficial environment, and freedom from ill-health and financial disaster[286].

The question I hear the reader raise is, how come the people of our globe do not choose the euphoric universe of the Tree of Life reality? Why remain glued to a chaotic universe of misery and misfortune? If this choice were as simple as it appears, no doubt mankind would have left this universe, which consists of everything one fears with trepidation each and every single day. The answer lies in and with the Dark Lord and his Death Star fleet.

Throughout recorded history, humankind has been divided into two basic categories, the coded groups of Israelites and the Erev Rav. The bloodstained history of religious conflict incorporates these two qualities. All religions are made up of those who accept the requirement of "Love thy neighbor" and those who purvey the energy-intelligence of evil. Intolerance, prejudice, and bigotry in the name of the Lord are manifestations of the antisocial face of the Dark Lord, the Erev Rav.[287]

Mankind alone will be the determining factor as to where the Aquarian Age takes us. Will the negative energy-intelligence of the Dark Lord, the Erev Rav, be subdued and harnessed for useful and peaceful purposes, revealing before our very eyes a beautiful cosmos of interdependency and inseparableness? Or will mankind fail to address the golden opportunity of this Aquarian Age, refusing the path of continuity with their arrogance, and thus perpetuate a world filled with cruelty and intolerance?

Persons lacking compassion, sensitivity and tolerance for others corrupt the cosmos with their negative energy-intelligence. To them we owe a world torn with violence. They are directly responsible for holocaust and destruction throughout the world regardless of the religion or purpose they profess to honor in its name. Murder remains murder, no matter what the rationale.

The Dark Lord runs a tight ship and maintains a strange hold on most of humanity. He dangles the bait of easy money, greed and quick shortcuts to fulfillment and immediate solutions. Therefore, he creates a social environment for mankind which is difficult to ignore despite something within us which cautions us to beware of the easy road to euphoria. Without the payment of restriction, we receive *nothing*.[288]

As defined by the Kabbalistic world view, the word *creation* is closely bound up and tied in with the concept of free will.[289] The creation of the observable physical world, including space and time, permitted man the corporeal expression of the

"Desire to Receive for Oneself Alone,"[290] the tool of the Dark Lord. This in turn gave us the opportunity to remove what is known in Kabbalah as "Bread of Shame".[291]

When we transform the Desire to Receive for the Self Alone to that of the Desire to Receive for the Sake of Sharing we have removed Bread of Shame and are now capable of handling, even channeling, the Lightforce of the Lord. Then, and only then, will Kabbalistic meditation and prayer successfully support our flight (*nes*, miracle) from the chaotic environment of the Tree of Knowledge to the ordered universe of the Tree of Life and all that its certainty implies.

This, then is the meaning and importance of pure awareness, the state of elevated consciousness. In that state we will find we are asking the right questions and coming to the right solutions. The answers that appear for us in our daily life are of a more permanent nature than the temporary relief to which we are accustomed. And more importantly, miracles no longer remain within our lexicon. The up and down swings in our lives occur less frequently if they do at all. We fully acknowledge and realize the presence of the Lightforce as the principle factor in our life's journey of certainty.

We are no longer brilliant or smart. We know and attribute our good fortune to the energy of the Lightforce which fortunately knows not of uncertainty, sickness, or financial chaos with which the Dark Lord attempts to brainwash our consciousness and prevent us from entering the Tree of Life reality. The Lightforce presses the right buttons for us so that we do not follow a path strewn with the debris of degenerative diseases, the pain and misery of broken relationships, and financial crises.

The *moment* we forget to acknowledge the Lightforce,

we create an opening[292] for the Dark Lord and his devastating fleet of innumerable beams of chaotic activity to enter into our lives. The Lightforce no longer is called upon to assist in our decisions. With the Lightforce receding, darkness overtakes our life journey as another conditional law of our universe is invoked, "Sin crouches at the door."[293]

We now should be prepared to comprehend the coded message which lies beneath the superficial, miraculous event, the splitting of the Red Sea. A good starting point for a correct investigation must land at the doorstep of the Zohar.

My dear Reader! I can understand your frustration, waiting for so long for the answer to the many questions raised concerning the event of the "Splitting of the Red Sea." However, to have answered the questions without addressing the quantum perspective of this event would have made me just as guilty as the scientists, economists, psychologists and other forecasters and researchers. We are now ready for a more comprehensive understanding of this matter with our level of consciousness raised and our awareness expanded.

An example of how quickly we begin to lower our consciousness and awareness, can be found in an important event and miracle described in the Bible.[294]

> And the whole Congregation of Israel, murmured against Moses and Aaron in the wilderness [when the bread was depleted, quotes Rashi]; And the Children of Israel said to them; Better had we died by the hand of the Lord in Egypt when we were seated around the pot of meat, when we ate bread to our fulfillment, for you have taken us out to this wilderness to put this entire congregation to

death through starvation.

Strange to hear these words coming from a nation that just witnessed and experienced the "miracle" of the ten plagues and the Splitting of the Red Sea. Could they and did they forget so quickly the power of the Lightforce of the Lord, the Omnipotent with whom everything and anything is possible? The Lightforce, which apparently controlled and stipulated the action of all physical corporeal matter, certainly could provide these people with bread.[295]

Only a mere few days earlier, when they had complained that there was no water to drink, did the Lightforce create a "miracle" especially for them and there appeared before them sweet water to drink.[296] Was it possible that they failed to remember this startling event in a matter of so short a span of time? And now they are back again with another similar complaint. This time for bread.

These tales, had they not appeared in the Bible, could be taken as a story from some novel. Too incredible to believe. And if these complaints are beyond reason, let us examine the latter part of this text where the narration begins to become unbelievable, and even diabolical on the part of the people.

> And the Lord said to Moses, "I will rain down for them bread from the heavens. And the people will go out and collect [the bread] for each day only [they shall not collect today or any day for tomorrow, *Mehilta*] so that I will prove whether they are going with my Torah [Lightforce] or not."[297]

Strange words coming from the Lord, if not totally incomprehensible. "Manna from heaven" should certainly suffice to convince the Israelites of the intervention by the Lord with His paranormal, supernatural powers. And yet the action Moses took implies that "raining manna from heaven" might not be sufficient to create among the Israelites that elevated state of consciousness which would recognize the presence, intervention and active participation of the Lightforce within the daily affairs of human existence.

Moses went on to request from the Israelites that they demonstrate their belief, understanding and connection with the Lord. This was to be achieved by having the Israelites collect the manna only for that day and to maintain faith in the Lord that tomorrow the manna will again appear.

Who in their right mind would continue to doubt whether the Lord had brought out this horde of slaves to enjoy the beneficence of the Promised Land or simply to die in the wilderness because of the lack of graves in Egypt? The raining of Manna from heaven was an event never before experienced by humankind nor any time thereafter. A further stipulation was necessary. They needed to erase "uncertainty" from their consciousness. There was no room for doubt.

When the time came to collect the "bread from the heavens" they were told that a complete surrender to the Lightforce presence was the only journey to "certainty." Despite their personal witnessing of so dramatic an event as "Manna from heaven," their connection with the Tree of Life and Lightforce certainty was not assured. Miracles by and within themselves do not change people. An altered state of consciousness cannot and will not be reached simply by an exposure to a miraculous event.

Miracles, whispers our soul consciousness,[298] occur each and every day whether or not we recognize them.[299] How many of us have come across a serious automobile accident that, had we arrived one moment earlier, might have involved us personally. The natural tendency is to slow down after passing the accident and possibly reflect on the idea that there *"but* for the grace of the Lord, go I." No sooner do we become involved in the activity of reaching our destination, the Tree of Knowledge reality, when we all but forget the incident.

Consequently, the supernatural phenomenon of "Manna from heaven" was soon forgotten. If the Israelites were not to make some personal effort to raise their consciousness, their communion with the Lord and certainty was not assured. The experience of personal participation is necessary. A display of the event means "being served on a silver platter." Like viewing TV, the full excitement comes to us on a silver platter, devoid of any effort on our part. Consequently, TV viewing has become a wasteland with the human mind being wasted away.

Let us briefly examine the in-depth reasoning behind this abnormal behavior of humankind. Wherein lies the *cause* behind this forgetfulness? Why do we not remember these spectacular events? What are the reasons for mankind to so quickly forget supernatural intervention? Why can't we maintain a belief of certainty that the Lord will "certainly" support and assist us tomorrow and into the future as he did today?

So long as we exist within the Tree of Knowledge reality of physicality, the Dark Lord reigns supreme. His infinite fleet and armada of uncertainty beliefs draw us down into the realm of uncertainty. This is the singular purpose and objective of his essence and being. The constant shifting of connection with the Tree of Life and Tree of Knowledge is what creates for us the illusionary idea that tomorrow remains uncertain.

We all experience miraculous interventions by the

Lightforce to remind us that at another level (Tree of Life) the future is assured with all its beneficence. No less than the *miracle* which broke and altered a material, physical event, we are accustomed to thinking that unless we create our bread, there is no bread. The raining of Manna from heaven alters the Dark Lord's conviction that we are so ready to accept.

Water's natural tendency to flow in our material world was changed by the "Splitting of the Red Sea." The Dark Lord's region of physical reality took a bitter defeat. However, the Dark Lord is aware of our body consciousness connected with the flesh and blood of our body. In our desire for material importance and greed, *we* revitalize the Dark Lord and His armada with renewed strength to continue misleading us into the belief that all there is for mankind is his "uncertainty" of the future.

Matters of ill-health, financial dilemma, broken relationships and misfortune are the realities of our human landscape. Two thousand years of war and devastation prove again and again that chaos is an inevitable participant in human existence.

Consequently, the Biblical passage under investigation begins to make some sense. The stipulation by the Lord for their unswerving commitment to "collect the Manna" for only a one day supply was a vital requirement. This would guarantee that tomorrow was here now with its full complement of order and fulfillment.

The verse provides a strikingly clear example of the short-lived impact of miracles. They surely are destined to be long gone and forgotten. These rare moments of revealed truth come and go, the purpose of which is a double edged sword. On the one hand, the stark, naked truth of the Tree of Life reality existence becomes known within the Tree of Knowledge domain.

Unfortunately, on the opposite side of this coin is poised the Dark Lord and his death fleet. They are fully committed to turn this opportunity of miracle revelation to one leading mankind along the path of delusional control over their lives.

As a result of the Dark Lord's efforts to intervene and assist in perpetuating the Tree of Knowledge, we forget the glimpse we had of the Tree of Life reality. We no longer consider the possibility that a Tree of Life existence consisting of "certainty" can be ours on a permanent basis. We have been programmed to accept the notion of "fast, fast, *temporary* instant relief" merely by consuming a pill without any requirement of effort on our part.

To raise our heads and see an advertisement reading "slow, slow, permanent relief" would prompt skepticism, if not disbelief. The idea of "instant" anything is what grabs us. The notion of "immediacy" is a key product in the illusion of time. Within the framework of the Tree of Life reality, immediate, past, future are all fragments and separations not in its domain. They simply do not exist. These concepts are obfuscations and reserved for those of us connected to the Tree of Knowledge universe.

In a demonstration of the overpowering force of the Dark Lord, the Biblical text continues with its in-depth penetration of man's journey through life's experience. Once again the Zohar's deciphering of the Bible brings to light the purpose and objective of the Bible, not one of a religious maze of unclear teachings, but rather, very clear markers along the path of man's day-by-day living encounters.

> And Moses said to them: "Do not leave over any
> of the Manna till the morning!" And they did not
> listen to Moses; they did leave over till morning

and the worms spoiled it and it dried up, and
Moses was angry with them. [300]

The miracle of "Manna from heaven" did not persuade
the Israelites nor influence them to recognize another dimension
in existence. They immediately fell prey to the Dark Lord's contention of "uncertainty," whether there will be another Manna
from heaven tomorrow.

In a crude manner, yet to the point, miracles may be
compared to a "fast fix" like an analgesic or surgery. For the most
part they occur infrequently. The reason for their rare appearance
and temporary stay lies precisely in our desire to receive relief
without investing the necessary time and effort to avoid and
remove Bread of Shame.[301]

The paradox[302] of chaos and misfortune, as opposed to
certainty and good fortune, is as beautiful and simple as the ris-
ing and setting of the sun. The paradox eliminates the illusion.
Upon experiencing pain, when requesting more, the pain leaves
us. This is a paradox that defies logic. When we suffer the pangs
of pain the natural tendency is to seek instant relief, certainly not
to increase our condition of discomfort.

However, the paradox is an essential, integral component
of the natural laws and principles of our universe. The filament
of a bulb[303] restricts the electric current but the result is illumination. Fasting and the exhalation of breath are restrictions of nour-
ishment and air but these restrictions improve our functioning,
demonstrating the paradox. Consequently, when requesting additional pain and discomfort, the paradox occurs. Contentment
and serenity are the results of desire to receive and maintain the
self for the self alone.

Why do we seek relief, even if it be only temporary? Who or what feels the pain? The soul, the part of us which is the Lightforce within us, certainly knows of no pain. The Lightforce and its Tree of Life reality belong to the certainty realm in our universe where only order and serenity exist.

Consequently, the aspect of *us* that senses and feels the illusionary reality of pain is our "body consciousness." The purpose of the discomfort is to achieve and manifest the *Tikune* process.[304] The pain we experience belongs to a cleansing process also known as *Tikune* (correction or cleansing). When the body feels pain, the pain is there for a temporary period to remove a prior lifetime activity of negativity. Once we endure the pain with the consciousness that we are repaying a prior debt, the pain will disappear almost immediately. There is no *purpose* for pain to continue if we accept the notion that its main function is to cleanse the dark side within ourselves.

However, if we do not display or feel a *genuine* satisfaction with the knowledge that pain and discomfort have come upon us to support and assist our *Tikune*, then our consciousness is not genuine or truthful. If we accept the idea of pain as a cleansing process, but keep looking over our shoulder to check if the Light is still there, or check the pain to see if it has diminished, then, in effect, we are demonstrating our uncertainty. For indeed, how does one know how long and to what extent the beneficial discomfort of pain is necessary to remove our negativity?

If this is our main concern, then why would one immediately reach for an analgesic, when this temporary relief and disappearance of pain also removes the cleansing agent that could erase any prior negativity. Why throw away the opportunity for elimination of our debts by seeking temporary relief, knowing all too well that the possessor of the debt will again demand payment?

It truly is simple. For this reason medical researchers can never nor will they ever find permanent solutions to the medical woes of mankind. Surgery or an analgesic is only a fast, temporary fix. This is not to say that an analgesic or surgery does not have an important place in medicine. The point that is being made is that we must have knowledge of pain and its purpose. Then, and only then, can we hope to achieve the *permanent* removal of body suffering in our time.

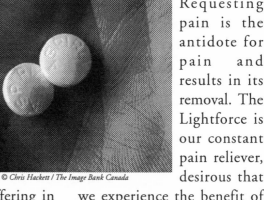

© Chris Hackett / The Image Bank Canada

The temporary relief is similar to the infrequent appearances of miracles. When the relief is not a result of our own effort and restriction, the doctrine of Bread of Shame[305] immediately becomes established, and the benefits of the Lightforce are lost.[306] Most individuals choose the easy way out, even when it includes surgery where there is nothing the patient need contribute.

As a general rule, what appears as less is more, and that which is more is less.[307] Removal of pain means asking for pain. Requesting pain is the antidote for pain and results in its removal. The Lightforce is our constant pain reliever, desirous that we experience the benefit of miracles day in and day out. However, what have we done or contributed to Its ever presence?

The appearance of miracles depends on independent human consciousness. We can and should experience the benefits of miracles each and every single day through the journey of our life's experience. We must understand and achieve a *consciousness* that miracles do *not* come about when the Lord has *the time* to perform these activities or *suddenly* is consumed with a compassion to assist mankind. Only when we come to this understanding do we access into this elevated consciousness, to the possibility of creating our own miracles. Miracles are only another way of describing connection and communion with the Lightforce.

Seeking out or accepting the opportunities for the removal of Bread of Shame is our ticket to the gate of Tree of Life. Once we access the domain of this reality level, the Lightforce becomes ever present. All that is then required is the connection by quantum prayer.

Consequently, when mankind questions the whereabouts of the Lord when He was needed most, the answer was and still is, He has been begging for two thousand years to permit His presence to become known and felt. However, the doctrine of "no coercion in spirituality" steps in, and the Lightforce must resign Itself to painfully permitting mankind to become dominated by the Dark Lord and his fleet.

If it depended on the desire of the Lightforce, there remains no question that It (Lightforce) would step in and bring a painful situation to an immediate, permanent solution. As stated in Scriptures: "My heart is aroused, I do not sleep."[308] But we, mankind, demand that the universal production be played our way. We insisted at the time of the Big Bang or beginning of Creation, that we could not tolerate the continuous flowing beneficence of the Lightforce without adequately *earning* this beneficence. We experienced Bread of Shame.

There are moments in our lives when we tend to forget

our stipulation to the Lord. We would rather forget *our* original choice of refusing to receive anything for nothing. During times of frustration and misfortune we certainly tend to override our original objection to the concept of Bread of Shame. However, the natural laws and principles of our universe were established by ourselves. *We* created the game plan.

Now that matters have gotten out of hand, with the Dark Lord apparently in total control, we prefer to change the rules in midstream. Forget the Bread of Shame doctrine mankind established. Even if we were to choose temporary relief with which the Lightforce is by far in agreement, the essential purpose of creation will not simply disappear.

The Lightforce is not controlled by man's decision to refuse to share the certainty of contentment and order. The desire of the Lightforce and Its intrinsic character of "desire to share" never ceases to be functional. The purpose of our existence, the removal of Bread of Shame, became firmly entrenched in the scheme of universal law. Proceeding against mankind's decision would not, in effect, be considered an act of sharing by the Lightforce.

When the cup of beneficence "runneth over," the compassion of the Lord takes on an aura of "Miracles." The display of sharing overtakes and overcomes the struggle and strife of mankind. However, this too must inevitably come to an end. Justifiable conflicts, where the aggressor is brought to his knees, have only been another stepping stone to further conflicts. Wars do not bring world conflict to an end. Bloodshed has never eliminated the suffering endured by mankind in its *Tikune* process, and it never will.

When these rare moments of relief and end to conflict

make their appearance, the cause behind this temporary breather is the beneficence of the Lightforce. Without a short, temporary intervention by the Lightforce mankind could not possess the stamina nor the will to continue its battle of removal of Bread of Shame with the elements of the Dark Lord.

Miracles then are a case of mistaken identity. They merely provide mankind with the opportunity to stop for a moment and reflect upon its existing, corrupted state of consciousness. We are given the chance to realize how little control we have over our destiny. Moreover, with a Kabbalistic view of our existence, the experience of these miracles provides us with another opportunity to reach out to the permanency of these miracles concealed within the Tree of Life reality. A permanent state of order, certainty and contentment can be ours for the asking. But, we must first earn it.

However, if we refuse to recognize the power of consciousness as our *only* tool in achieving communion with the Lightforce and all that it implies, then *knowledge*, so essential in making the connection to the Lightforce, will fail to support and assist our attempts at connecting with the Lord.

In this Age of Aquarius, we must *abandon* the idea of a *merciful* Lord who occasionally provides us with a taste of a miracle that removes near chaos and destruction. Man's experience and historical data indicate that we have experienced more chaotic events in our past two thousand years of existence than moments of order and fulfillment in our lives. This certainly does not echo of a sharing, caring and compassionate Lord.

That the Lord constantly waits in the wings of the stage of our unfolding lives, states the Zohar, is the true description of a compassionate Lord. His desire to share His beneficence at *all* times is closer to the truth. His observation of mankind's pursuit to achieve freedom from financial uncertainty and failure, broken relationships and ill health only strengthens His desire to see a change in the pattern of human behavior. He almost goes begging for his created beings to access into the reality of the Tree of Life.

It is for this reason that Kabbalah in our Aquarian Age has become so widespread, to remove the frustration and helplessness that have been man's trademark almost since the time of creation, to instill within the consciousness of all human beings the idea that miracles are not the work of the Lord alone. While the Lightforce of the Lord and Its Tree of Life reality are the instruments for the constant appearance of miracles, we must come to a state of elevated consciousness and pure awareness which recognizes that in the final analysis it is our own conscious connection with the Lightforce that will determine when miracles shall occur. And miracles can become a permanent part of our landscape. However, we dare not forget, the constant events of miracles in our lives cannot become a living reality if we assume that we *do not* have the power to make them happen. A positive attitude and consciousness are the first prerequisite as evidenced by the first precept revealed to the Israelites in Egypt, "Know the Lord."

Where do we find any indication that a *total surrender* of our satanic-fed four-percent mind consciousness is required? This idea almost smacks of occultism. "Surrender your mind, give me your brain" are expressions reverberating throughout the cult movement.

However, from the Zoharic text soon to be quoted, the notion of surrender takes on another meaning completely. Firstly, it will become self-evident that in the Zoharic expression of "total surrender" never is there any thought of surrender to another person. The concept expressed by the Zohar is that our four-percent mind consciousness is only an expression of our limiting, self-defeating ego. The Zohar desires that we regain the potential ninety-six percent of our mind capacity and capability.

The system by which we can recapture our almost total consciousness is to surrender to the awareness that our four-percent consciousness is controlling our thoughts and actions preventing our access into the Lightforce. When the Zohar discusses the idea of "surrender," in no way does this imply an attempt to eliminate the presence of our limited four-percent consciousness. On the contrary, the four-percent consciousness serves as our tool for the removal and elimination of Bread of Shame, not the removal or elimination of our conscious four-percent mind.

Without our limited, egotistical four-percent brain, we could simply ease into the domain of the Tree of Life. That would constitute Bread of Shame. Therefore, mankind must work and make an effort to overcome this ego-minded four-percent consciousness whose single purpose is to divert our attention away from a communion with the Lightforce. The presence of our ego encourages us to believe we have total control until such time that we approach the inevitable experience of chaos and disaster. Even when financial chaos strikes, our four-percent satanic ego cunningly convinces us that we actually are in control, if we had only avoided some silly, stupid decision which brought about our chaotic circumstances. Little do we realize that control never belonged to the four-percent domain of our consciousness.

Consequently, in our discussion of surrendering our conscious mind, the implication is to be clearly understood as one of taking complete *control* over our satanic-driven four-percent mind. This is the notion that paradoxically brings control.

Remove the illusionary thought of *control* of the four-percent mind, then, and only then, do we indeed achieve control.

For control lies only with the Lightforce. The definition of control requires a quantum process touching the full spectrum of universal activities. Without quantum control there is no control. Without quantum prayer there is no connection to the quantum control of the Lightforce.

And now, the Israelites are caught between the waters of the flowing Red Sea in front of them and the Egyptians not too far behind them. The threat appears quite obvious, drowning in the Red Sea or death at the hands of their Egyptian pursuers. What remains for them to do? In times of need and despair even nonbelievers have turned to the Lord. Even the Israelites, the constant complainers with little faith in the Lord, began to pray to the Almighty.

Then the question that must be raised at this time is why the Lord responds to Moses with the question, "Why do you cry out to Me?"[309] To whom else should the Israelites address their problems and plights if not to the Lord?

Furthermore, states the Zohar,[310] What is meant by the Lord's response "and they shall travel?"[311] Where are they to travel? The sea was there in front of them. Surely they would drown in the surging waters of the Red Sea.

The meaning of the verse is as follows: "Why do you cry out to Me?" Since the Israelites had achieved an elevated state of consciousness to that of *Tiferet*, the Tree of Life reality, there was no further need for prayer or to "cry out to Me." Drowning or dying here in the wilderness was no longer an expectation within their newly achieved reality of the Tree of Life.

The secret meaning and internal interpretation of the words "and they shall travel" relates to their existing state of consciousness. Considering the presence of the Lightforce and the Tree of Life reality which was now reigning supreme, there was no further need for any action. *Travel on course*, there needn't be any fear. The Lightforce is now in control. Concepts like drowning or dying in the wilderness no longer belong within the lexicon of their life's journey.[312]

The lack of, or no control which existed at their former level of existence, the Tree of Knowledge level, was left behind. They had already jumped to the parallel universe of existence, the Tree of Life reality. Having surrendered the Tree of Knowledge consciousness, the ideas connected with that four-percent consciousness no longer existed for them.

By the same token, the concepts and tools of our lower (four-percent) consciousness cannot grasp the idea that there is no past, present or future. Neither can it grasp the reality of certainty which is associated with the Tree of Life universe, the ninety-six percent of our consciousness. This might be compared to a man born blind. All explanations connected with the idea of light remain concealed and are not understood by this blind man. His level of consciousness cannot absorb the "taken for granted" concept of light.

Consequently, the Lord's question was a reminder to the Israelites that they had achieved an upper level (Tree of Life) state of consciousness. One must discard or *surrender* those notions back to where they originally came from, back to the Satanic world of the Dark Lord and his Death Star fleet, the tools of our lower consciousness. Ego, the most formidable armada of the Dark Lord takes mankind back to the feeling and sensation of the "I." "I" accomplished this or that, "I" have been hurt by the insensitivity of others; "I" believe or "I" understand. These words or concepts do not smack of the quantum level of all. "We," on the other hand, includes everyone and everything.

By limiting our consciousness to *me* rather than *we*, we remove ourselves from possible quantum control over the cause and destiny of our lives. As previously explained, if we do not make our connections to the Lightforce, then quantum control eludes us and we remain with limited, illusionary control over the journey of existence. For this reason, the lower level of consciousness is referred to as illusionary. The perfect specimen of health fades away into the tomorrow of illness. Here today, gone tomorrow. Financial stability, a trademark of the financial world ultimately, if not in this generation then in future generations, disappears as the wind. Almost as if stability had never existed. Illusionary!

This is the world of existence that most of us experience. Therefore, the term "illusionary" is applied to this type or manner of life's existence. This has been and is the trademark of our civilization. Programmed by the environment around us, one finds it extremely difficult "to let" go of our illusionary habits.

Herein lies precisely the game plan of the Dark Lord. How can we surrender or let go of the consciousness, albeit limited, that we are familiar with and come to recognize that this is our only salvation? If we do not hold on with dear life to the little that we do possess, if we were to surrender the familiar consciousness and materialism, how can we be certain that all that we need is ours to have, and more importantly, to keep?

If the price of a ticket to a large fortune is the surrendering of a small fortune, no one in their right mind would hesitate to purchase that ticket. However, the Dark Lord reminds us of the *uncertainty* or the lack of assurance or conviction that a large fortune actually lies in store for us.

Just take a look at the cunning Dark Lord. He convinces us of the *uncertainty* of achieving greater success by surrender, as if the little that we now maintain or have is ours for sure or *certain*. Therefore we choose the temporary, knowing full well that our temporary acquired health (no headache) will shortly disappear. We hold on to this notion "with dear life," at the expense of possibly losing it *all*, along with the little that we *think* we do possess.

The certainty realm of the Tree of Life is not a "New Age" concept. This idea came with the scriptural package of the Bible and its eternal significance deciphered by the Zohar. Has not mankind, after thousands of years of life's experience, learned the lesson? The world we consciously know and observe around us is temporary, non-fulfilling and filled with chaos and turmoil. How long must we wait before we attempt another course in our journey through life?

The Israelites, after securing a beachhead within the Tree of Life reality, nevertheless fell into the awaiting trap of the Dark Lord. Israelites, why have you surrendered your consciousness? Look around you. Do you not see the observable reality of your imminent peril, the water in front of you and the Egyptians in the rear?

These dilemmas and tactics of the Dark Lord have plagued mankind as long as we can remember. Then, we may ask, what hope lies for the future of mankind. If humankind has been unsuccessful for so long a time, how do we expect to alter and change the course of history and individual destiny?

The response of the Zohar provides mankind with the

knowledge and answer to this formidable question. The Zohar states:[313]

> In the days of the Age of Aquarius, there will no longer be the necessity for one to request of his neighbor teach me wisdom, as it is written,[314] One day they will no longer teach every man his neighbor and every man his brother, saying know the Lord. For they shall all know *Me* from the youngest to the oldest of them.

The Zohar clearly intimates that the Messianic era will usher in a period of unprecedented knowledge to the layperson. Messianism is bound up and dependent upon true knowledge, the wisdom of Kabbalah. Knowledge originating within the software of the Zohar permits mankind to access into quantum knowledge of the universe.

The possibility of raising our level of consciousness becomes certain by installing this universal software onto our own particular mind computer. The science of the Kabbalah does answer many of the enigmatic aspects of nature, yet it still remains elegantly simple.

> And the Lord said to Moses, ... lift up your rod and stretch out your hand over the sea and divide it... and the Israelites went into the midst of the sea on dry ground.[315]

These words came and were spoken by the Lord to Moses. However, when it came time to actualize the spoken word of the Lord, the text changes somewhat and continues to evolve as a concept defying rational logic.

And Moses stretched out his hand over the sea
and the Lord led the sea by a strong east wind all
night, and [made] turned the sea to dry land and
then the waters were split.[316]

The commentators raise the obvious question.[317] The
verse should have read in reverse: "And the waters were split and
the sea was turned to dry land," inasmuch as the sea could not
have turned to dry land if the sea was not split beforehand.

What apparently emerges from this abstruse and concealed verse is the notion of mind over matter. When Moses
raised his hand to split the Red Sea, the consciousness of Moses
already caused the sea to split. In a quantum perspective of
nature, information flows between two points or two separate
entities instantly. The sea *knew* immediately the bidding consciousness of Moses and therefore responded by an instant reaction of its own consciousness to become split.

In the true reality realm, where separation and differences
do not exist, consciousness and materialism operate within the
definitive guidelines of cause and effect. The cause controls and
the effect is the result. The mind is considered to be the cause
and the material the effect.

This idea has already found its roots in scientific phenomena. When throwing a rock at a glass window, prior to the
rock reaching and smashing the window, the window has already
begun to show signs of cracking. Somehow the conscious mind
of the rock thrower has already touched and penetrated the internal consciousness of the window itself.

This concept, while scientifically researched, tested and
proven beyond doubt, nevertheless remains outside the confines

of the layperson's consciousness. The reason is the dilemma facing the scientist. Why can't he walk through the front door of his home despite his forgetting to take the key with him when he left the house in the morning?

However, in this Age of Aquarius, all of mankind will have the opportunity to access into the quantum hardware of knowledge and information. This conclusion of the Zohar also applies to those scientists with an elevated state of consciousness. Once they surrender their limited notions of Dark Lord consciousness, they can tap the vast fountains of knowledge of the Tree of Life quantum computer.

How beautiful and simple are the Aquarian and Messianic concepts of the Zohar. The only people left out and deprived of the quantum knowledge of the cosmos are those who cannot surrender their Dark Lord consciousness because of ego or distorted logic. In either case, whether we access into the Tree of Life or Tree of Knowledge realities, our consciousness belongs to the robotic state of each reality.

The free will that exists is, from a Kabbalistic perspective, the choice of either succumbing to our egotistical reality of the four-percent Dark-Lord consciousness or choosing the Tree of Life cassette, the prepared life journey of certainty and fulfillment. Of course, I am prepared for those diehard egocentric individuals who will reject outright the opportunity to surrender their out-of-control uncertainty. The enjoyment and sensation of thinking, albeit robotically, that *we* made the choice of uncertainty and misfortune, far outweigh the benefits of the certainty of the Tree of Life reality.

As sick or stupid as this choice seems to be, this conclusion is the one mankind has chosen since the beginning of time.

There is no argument with recorded history. What these same people might argue about is whether there is another choice for humankind to access into. The Zohar states, in no uncertain terms, that there is. Furthermore, declares the Zohar, the Aquarian Age will assist all of mankind to achieve an elevated state of consciousness to enjoy the simple and beautiful state of our universe.

The Splitting of the Red Sea came about by virtue of an elevated state of consciousness within the Israelites. Furthermore, they were convinced of their ability to control the material state of consciousness — in this case, the matter of water. For precisely this reason, the Bible injects the additional instruction of Moses to the Israelites, "travel" or "jump into the sea."[318]

When Moses raised his rod, he made *manifest* his Tree of Life consciousness. For Moses, the sea had already been split by virtue of his state of consciousness and neither the sea nor the Egyptians created any problem for his welfare. The Lightforce/Tree of Life reality never abandons those who cleave to it. Chaos and destruction are not trademarks of the Lightforce. Moses never had any doubts as to his own personal survival. He was already destined never to falter in his connection with the Lightforce and Tree of Life reality.

The Moses connection is clearly indicated in another one of the Biblical codes so grossly misinterpreted.

"And the man Moses was extremely humble, more so than any other man that was ever on the face of the earth."[319] A splendid tribute to the man Moses. However, when we consider that the writer of the Bible, was Moses, one must place in question the tribute to Moses. Sounds awfully strange for one to describe himself as "very humble," full of humanity, and assume the reader will accept a tribute of this sort in all earnest. If one strives to achieve humility and become humble, the person certainly will not do it with a sign around his neck stating, "I am a humble person."

Then how would Moses take the liberty to write about himself and state his accomplishment at having achieved the distinction of being the most humble person that ever inhabited the face of this earth? This isn't the manner by which those with humility behave. On the contrary, climbing the ladder of humbleness requires the individual to shun accolades that may come his or her way for fear of arousing the egocentricity forever latent with all of us.

Humility represents and portrays the intrinsic character of the Lightforce, one of *sharing consciousness.* The individual makes every attempt to divert attention away from him/herself for fear of emulating the "desire to receive for the self alone," the satan-consciousness of the four percent of our self. To the extent and degree that one achieves humility, the connection with the Tree of Life reality and Lightforce is enhanced.

Consequently, the intent and purpose of the verse under discussion is to examine the state of communion between Moses and the Lightforce. Moses, states Scriptures, had reached the level of consciousness where he, Moses, no longer expressed a thought originating within Moses. Rather, Moses was a complete and perfect expression of the Lightforce, unadulterated by the satan-consciousness of the four-percent Tree of Knowledge illusionary reality.[320]

Humility is not a state of mind. Rather, to be humble is a Lightforce state of consciousness, one in which we completely surrender to the infinite, quantum reality of Lightforce. The words echoing from the mouth of Moses were not the thoughts of Moses but rather of the Lightforce.

Reflect for a moment on the words and sentences flowing from our mouth. Are we in touch with our conscious mind as to what and how our thoughts originated in our mind? We rarely experience any contact between our mind and our thoughts. Unless we decide to give a subject careful thought and consideration, our conversations rarely take on any significance, especially when our discussion turns toward the weather.

The question we must ask ourselves is how did these sentences originate and who brought them to the surface in our consciousness? Our consciousness, whether the state of mind we are aware of, or the subconscious level we are unaware of, emanates from a prepared cassette-producing instrument. If the spoken statements result in greater rewards than expected, rarely will we attribute any of this to the Lightforce.

The level of Lightforce consciousness enjoyed by Moses enabled him to cause the Red Sea to split, but only with regard to himself. In fact Moses split the Red Sea long before the sea became visibly split. If this miracle were to be realized by the Israelites, they would require the same state of consciousness, that is, a connection with the Tree of Life reality. This the Israelites had achieved as the Zohar stated. Therefore, the Lord responded to their fears, "why do the Israelites cry out to Me?", their consciousness was already connected with the Lightforce.

Therefore, Moses was told by the Lord to command the Israelites, "Travel," jump into the sea, which provided the second stage of the necessary requirement. Make the sea split at the corporeal level of existence. Reveal the already existing reality of "mind over matter" and the stipulation that the Lord established at the time of Creation. The creation or manifestation of miracles is an act that only mankind makes manifest.

The Lord, at the time of Creation, had set the wheels in motion. He placed the Tree of Knowledge reality of existence where it properly belongs, to be subject to the Tree of Life existence where no chaos, destruction and devastation belong, where death takes a holiday. The fear of the Egyptians from behind and the seas in front were all part of the Tree of Knowledge reality. They were totally illusionary, albeit, for most of us a hard reality.

However, once the second requirement — the physical demonstration that our mind consciousness is truly with the Lightforce, where the rational, illusionary mind of ours is eliminated — then, what some people consider to be a miracle of the Lord, the event of the Red Sea, becomes a mere subsequent effect of our Lightforce consciousness, a result of *our own* level of Lightforce consciousness.

The rational mind of the Israelites spoke out with thoughts of death, chaos and destruction being inevitable: either death at the hands of the Egyptians or drowning by the sea. Jumping in meant inescapable death by drowning.

However, by entering the waters of the Red Sea, they demonstrated their unflinching conviction of their connection with the Lightforce. While the rational mind could observe the obvious conclusion of death by drowning, their communion with the Lightforce could not and would not consider any aspect of chaos, including drowning. These were concepts that belonged to the illusionary level of the Tree of Knowledge existence.

The results were inevitable. The Lord already expressed and manifested the stipulation. Man could, if he so desired, control every aspect of his destiny and future. All manner and forms of uncertainty and chaos that mankind experiences do not belong to the Tree of Life reality level.

Every person has a given, natural birthright to the pursuit of happiness. One must merely find the right road and maintain a proper level of consciousness. Falling from the "good graces of the Lord" means we have chosen another level of existence, in this case, our choice to exist and live in the Tree of Knowledge reality of chaos and uncertainty.

Before closing this important and revealing chapter, let us examine another verse[321] contained in the narration of the splitting of the Red Sea. "And the Egyptians shall know that I am the Lord when I become exalted by Pharaoh, his chariots and horsemen." However, reflecting upon a verse mentioned earlier in this Biblical text, the verse under consideration creates some confusion. "And Moses said to the nation: do not fear, remain steadfast and observe the salvation of the Lord that He shall perform for you today. For as you see the Egyptians today, you shall no longer ever see them again."[322]

A contradiction apparently exists between these two verses If, as the second verse seems to indicate, the Egyptians will not survive the event of the splitting of the Red Sea, then how will the honor of the Lord become exalted by the Egyptians as stated in the first verse just mentioned, when they no longer are counted among the living? If there are no survivors among the Egyptians, how will future generations transmit the truth of this historical event?

A good starting point for our investigation lies in the Zohar which cautions the reader of the Bible that the Bible represents no more than the physical expression of the forces that exist and govern in our universe. The Zohar states that if one observes and reads the Bible as stories and parables without recognizing its true, metaphysical significance, then the observance and the reading are, like straw, lifeless.[323]

Consequently, when considering these two verses, we cannot, nor should we, interpret them superficially. The written word is to the essential spiritual meaning as the body is to the soul; the spiritual meaning is the internal aspect, the written word (or the body) is the vessel for its revealment.[324] Considering the concept of "Egyptian," let us return to the Zohar for an in-depth explanation of the essential meaning of this word that on the surface apparently refers to the Middle Kingdom of yester-year. At the same time, let us not forget, even for a moment, that the Bible is not a document for the recording of history, nor a compendium for the establishment of religion in general, nor of the Jewish religion in particular.

> AND IT CAME TO PASS IN THE COURSE OF THOSE MANY DAYS...[325] Rabbi Joshua of Saknin said: It was the end of the exile in Egypt. The many days of exile came to an end as it is written "And the King of Egypt died." What does this mean? The supernal angel of Egypt was dethroned from his exalted position and fell from grace. Therefore, the verse states: "And the King of Egypt died," inasmuch as lowering one's former position is considered as death.
>
> Said Rabbi Yehudah: It is as Rabbi Joshua of Saknin said. For as long as the supernal angel of Egypt was given control over the Israelites, even their pleas could not penetrate and reach the realm of the Lord. This is indicated in the follow-

ing verse, "and their pleas went up to the Lord!"

Said Rabbi Isaac in the name of Rabbi Joshua: Come and see. So long as there exists the ruler-ship of any nation above (the supernal minister of that nation), there shall exist the rulership of the physical nation below. The moment the minister-ing angel of that nation is removed, rulership of the nation below is also removed.[326]

Here again, the Zohar is interpreting the words of the Bible as referring to a deeper level of meaning than might imme-diately be apparent. The Biblical name given to Egypt, *Mitzraim*, comes from the root word *mizar*, meaning narrow, squeezed, compressed and restricted. The power of the Egyptians had squeezed out the Lightforce, the quantum positive energy of the universe. This was the reason why the Egyptians were capable of enslaving and dominating the nations of the entire world.

Consequently, what seems to emerge from this startling Zohar is the Kabbalistic view that the battles and wars that take place between men on the physical level do not originate at this corporeal level. The real battles and conflicts, in whatever man-ner or form they take, originate and are the results of struggles between forces on the metaphysical level of existence.[327]

Therefore, if mankind desires to establish "peace on earth, goodwill toward men," force — on our familiar level of existence — will never achieve this most sought after objective. We might temporarily reach these goals, but reflecting on past recorded his-tory, these achievements have always been short lived, and mankind's dreams shattered.

The Zohar strongly urges us to address our attention to

the metaphysical level of existence where the action begins and ends.

The Kabbalah furnishes the essential tools and necessary information towards making these connections with the realm of true reality, the Tree of Life level of existence.

If we can move the forces of the Tree of Life to dominate the "good and evil" level of the Tree of Knowledge existence, then a *permanent positive* result will inevitably come forth. This is the interpretation provided by the Zohar on the verse quoted previously.

> Stand fast and observe the salvation of the Lord! There is no need to wage war, for the Lightforce shall conduct the war on your behalf.... As it is written: The Lord shall do war on your behalf and you shall remain quiet!

> Come and see! In that night (the night of the Exodus) the Lightforce gathered his army of various ministering angels and they began to judge the Israelites on their merit. And if the energy forces of Abraham, Isaac and Jacob were not brought into the scenario and pray (make their presence felt), they would not have found their salvation.

> Rabbi Yehudah said: The energy force of central column symbolized by Jacob, the Patriarch, came forth and acted as the protectorate over the Israelites.[328]

What seems to emerge from the Zohar is that once the

Dark Lord had been defeated, and in the case of the Israelites at Exodus, devastated, he had been permanently laid to rest. This was indicated in the verse by "you shall no longer see the Egyptians ever again."[329] The reason for the permanency of their efforts was directly due to their waging battle where it counts most, on the metaphysical stage of the realm of reality.

The Israelites employed the awesome power of the Lightforce in achieving lasting victory over the Egyptians. They *knew* how to destroy the Dark Lord of Egypt permanently. In fact, the destruction of the Middle Kingdom of Egypt brought down the full glory of Egypt, never again to regain her place among the towering mighty nations of the world. This was not a question of belief or a matter of the Lord performing miracles.

Another indication of their performance to achieve the impossible against the Egyptians and the sea is indicated by the following Zohar.[330] "Said Rabbi Shimon: Praiseworthy is the portion of the Israelites that a shepherd such as Moses was among them. As it is written,[331] 'and He remembered the days of old, Moses and his people.'"

The reason why the stipulation was necessary regarding the "splitting of the Red Sea" event and not on other occasions such as the splitting of waters by the sages of the Talmud[332] and the splitting of the Jordan River[333] by Joshua, is precisely because of the presence of Moses among the Israelites.

The original stipulation provided mankind with the opportunity to become masters of their physical environment and surroundings. This awesome power transmitted to the kingdom of man was first indicated in the Bible when Adam gave names to the animals.[334] Prior to the splitting of the Red Sea, the Israelites became the *first group* of people with the capability to acquire quantum control over the whole of the universe. Moses shared with the Israelites the quantum secret of seventy-two names,[335] by which they, the Israelites, now in possession of the connecting channels to the awesome power of the Lightforce, could by themselves, split the Red Sea — hence the command by the Lord to the Israelites: "travel."

Furthermore, the effective control now displayed by the Israelites also included the quantum control of time. The manifestation of the Lightforce over the forces of darkness was their assurance that victory over the Dark Lord and his armada of death star fleets was not a temporary state of relief. Quantum, as its name indicates, included yesterday as it does tomorrow.

Thus, the Biblical text states: "and the Egyptians shall know that I am the Lord (Lightforce) when I become honored (exalted) by Pharaoh, his chariots and horsemen" now begins to make sense. Although, the nation of Egypt will survive the disaster of the splitting of the Red Sea, they no longer will possess the awesome negative power that could enslave the entire world. This force of the Middle Kingdom of Egypt was now permanently displaced by the awesome power of the Lightforce.

Evidence of the quantum effect of the Lightforce and Its presence as a permanent deterrent to the negative rulership of the Dark Lord in Egypt is the Biblical declaration,[336] "for as you see the Egyptian *today*, only *today* shall you see them thus, for you shall *never again* see them thus." Scripture makes it perfectly clear that when the Lightforce by virtue of the seventy-two names, became expressed and manifest by the Israelites, this force was not limited or bound up with the restriction of time. Once the Lightforce eliminated the power of the Dark Force and his fleet's destruction, they no longer could remain as a viable force in the future.

On our terrestrial, mundane level, occupation forces of today become the vanquished conquerors of yesterday. Empires have come and gone with the wind only to reappear at some future date. Germany has hit the dust many times in the past, only to reemerge as a world power. The see-saw domination of nations have become part of our historical landscape.

Not so with Egypt, states Scripture. Once the Lightforce of the Tree of Life made Its presence felt, Egypt would *never* again make its reentry into the world of nations as it once was. The effect of the Lightforce is one of a permanent nature. The force of the Tree of Life operates at the metaphysical level. Once having defeated the ministering angel and lord of the upper realm of the Egyptian nation, Egypt would no longer survive nor ever return as a major player among powers.

The timeless evidence of Egypt's failure to maintain its foothold and glory which once was demonstrated by the Middle Kingdom of Egypt, bears witness to Scripture's prophecy, "you shall *never* again see them thus." The significance of this passage lies not in the scriptural testimonial concerning the Middle Kingdom of Egypt. What does emerge from the *coded* event, the splitting of the Red Sea, is that when the knowledge of the seventy-two names is put to the extreme test, the result is one of a permanent nature.[337] Temporary relief simply does not exist in the lexicon of the Lightforce nor within the framework of Kabbalistic knowledge. The Tree of Life reality does not associate with, nor is it in any way connected with, the illusionary vocabulary employed within our terrestrial realm of the Tree of Knowledge.

Consequently, the stipulation and its significance, concerning the event of the Red Sea was established at the time of Creation. That water was to be subject to the command and demands of man was, of necessity, established at the time of

Creation. Similar to the seed of the tree which mothers endless routes and paths for its branches, this stipulation concerning water brought every form of its manifestation under the control of mankind. Whether water makes its appearance as a cup of water, ocean, sea or river, because the stipulation was established at seed level, Creation, the stipulation weaves its way through every aspect of its proliferation.

Obviously, the control at seed level also includes the extension and state of time. The future is already included within the seed. Time for us is but an illusionary perspective of fragmentation. That there is a tomorrow as well as a yesterday cannot be, and is not, considered within the seed. The notion of tomorrow certainly cannot be considered when we observe the seed with its potential root and subsequent branch. Both appear in the seed at the same time.

Time is, in fact, a sequence of events. A definite or infinite number of connected phases branching from each other is the order of cause and effect. As the seed contains the root and the root contains the branches, the root of control by man that was to become manifestly expressed in physical terms, of necessity must have been contained within the seventy-two energy intelligences[338] which were given physical terms as the letters of the Aleph Beth.

The revelation of the seventy-two names and how they were to be applied toward reaching man's objective of control over his destiny was revealed by Moses just prior to the critical event of the Red Sea. Through these coded names mankind could tap the miraculous powers within the Lightforce. The codes enable man to harness the power of the Lightforce and remove any road-blocks that stand in the way of health and happiness.

Therefore, it becomes quite evident, that the stipulation at the time of Creation came about for the express purpose of providing the essential tools by which mankind, once having acquired the knowledge of how to use them, could in fact create their own miracles. There no longer was the need to call upon the Creator to assist with newly born or formed miracles. They were all there at the time of Creation. All that was left was for man to make the Lightforce become physically expressed. This was the chore left to man.

Whereas, the science of physics has no choice but to pursue a pathway of probabilities, the Kabbalist, unlike the scientist does not suffer from a plague of uncertainty. Kabbalists travel the same sure road followed by the celestial bodies. The sun and moon have never been uncertainties for us in our observations of them. They rise and set with predictable outcomes and precision.

This is quite the opposite of the wild guesses made by scientists while expressing contempt for the Biblical description of our universe. Kabbalah holds out the promise of a real science of the future. A valid futurology is indeed possible despite the fact that the future appears more complex and unpredictable with every passing moment.

To provide what I consider the most lucid example given by science concerning their dilemmas: in May 1989 there was an announcement made by astrophysicist George Smoot of the Lawrence Berkeley Laboratory in California. He announced that they had found the Lord's handwriting at the edge of space. On Nov. 18, 1989, Nasa launched a $160 million satellite to seek the memoirs of Genesis.

COBE (Cosmic Background Explorer) measures the nearly uniform sea of microwaves that bathes all of space. The microwave sea seemed incredibly smooth. The theorists were desperate to discover clumps. If energy and matter are spread across the heavens so evenly, how could particles have ever clumped together to form clusters and great galaxies?

In the summer of 1991, their dream came true. As Smoot's team pored over some 430 million measurements radioed back from the satellite, they glimpsed the discovery of a lifetime. They found the "imprints of tiny ripples in the fabric of spacetime put there by the primeval explosion," says Smoot. "These are 15 billion-years-old fossils created at the *birth* of the universe." To be *precise*, the wrinkles date from just 300,000 years after the big bang, "as close as we are *ever* going to get to creation itself" says UC's Primack. They *may* show how the universe evolved after the big bang.

Notice the glaring contradiction concerning so important a matter as the "beginning" of Creation. The Big Bang theory, while the only available explanation as to how it all started, has never been totally substantiated. What did they find? "They found the imprints of tiny ripples in the fabric of spacetime put there by the primeval explosion." One could assume from the foregoing explanation that physical proof of the big bang has finally been established. By their use of the words "primeval explosion," they lead us to believe they have finally unraveled the mystery of the way it all began.

And then "to be precise" they continue to elaborate upon their new findings by stating that the new data concerning "the wrinkles date from *just* 300,000 years after the big bang." This statement obviously indicates that their new findings are not connected to the primeval explosion but only a mere 300,000 years after.

Finally, when they are prepared to serve us dessert, they

state with convincing and very persuasive authoritative language that this is "as close as we are ever going to get to Creation itself." What seems to emerge from all this is that scientists, in their search for the truth, finds their groping fingers inadequate to arrive at definitive findings.

To further strengthen the case for Kabbalah, Einstein's Theory of Relativity destroyed the idea of universal time, and of an absolute past, present and future. Einstein himself never did fully explain why universal time no longer exists. After all, to understand the "way" and "why" of things was not then and, unfortunately, still is not within the province of science.

Considering the foregoing, there is a need to understand the Kabbalistic concept of cause and effect. Every effect has its cause whether or not we can determine the causes. The Kabbalist recognized the futility of linking cause only with an observable effect. Doing so has brought about the uncertainties that plague the scientist. However, the world of uncertainty as introduced by the noted physicist, Werner Heisenberg, belongs only to the world of physics. In the realm of metaphysics, reality is seen unwinding along a precise, predetermined route that must and will lead to an unalterable final state.

In our confused, crisis-ridden generation are we in some way better suited to achieve purer awareness and states of elevated consciousness? The answer, confirms the Zohar, is an emphatic yes. The peoples of the entire world, who for so long have been shut out from the enlightenment reserved for the few will, in our Age of Aquarius, access into the wellspring of heretofore concealed, simplified answers to the enigmas of life's experiences.

We shall all benefit from its teachings which can erase the doubts and uncertainties that beset daily living. Just what is it that places its teachings on a unique pedestal? The Kabbalistic world view reflects the innate harmony of our universe provided we can raise our consciousness to observe it.

Rather than place the problems of society within a symptomatic frame of reference, the Kabbalah cuts through to the basic problem which spells out in terms of "why." Why has mankind turned to drugs — medicinal or abusive — in the first place? Why is the individual more vulnerable today to outside influences than ever before? Why has language suddenly become a banner for hatred among people? In fact, why do people feel an affinity with those who speak their language? Physical circumstances never lead to a satisfactory answer.

An expanded awareness and elevated consciousness, states the Zohar,[339] is the mysterious message of Kabbalah. With our sights set on the "high road" of reality, we can overcome all obstacles. It is simply a matter of disengaging from the darkness of satan-consciousness and illusion and becoming consciously connected with the reality of the Lightforce.

In this Age of Aquarius, the consciousness and realization that mankind has been duped has been raised to a level never before experienced. The resignation of mankind in its dream toward a world which includes peace on earth, good will toward man, has begun to reverse itself. Never before in history have the people begun to take matters into their own hands as they are doing in our day. Rather than surrender their future and place it in the hands of others, the people have begun to express their own desires and determinations.

The Lightforce has made its intentions clear to the world in this day of redemption. It no longer desires to remain a passive force, only to be used when called upon to do so. Consequently, to remain within the confines of universal law which decrees the doctrine of "no coercion in spirituality," the Lightforce has embarked upon another avenue to find expression.

The Age of Aquarius is the age of information and knowledge. This has become increasingly evident by the radical changes that have overtaken the long sleeping doctrines of the scientific community. The outpouring of knowledge within the scientific community in the past seventy years has out-paced and surpassed the amount and significance of scientific knowledge over the past two thousand years.

These same past seventy years have given birth to Kabbalistic knowledge and information never before accessible to the people, including those not knowledgeable in Biblical studies. The onward march toward *permanent* freedom from want and suffering has never been so close to realization nor within the grasp of all mankind as it is today. The snowball has come-a-rolling. There is no stopping it now.

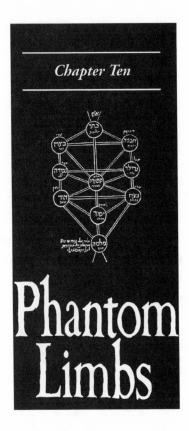

Chapter Ten

Phantom Limbs

THE AMPUTEE'S SENSE OF THE PRESENCE OF THE AMPUTATED limb is most extraordinary. The phantom limb may seem more substantial than an actual limb, especially if it hurts. The sense of reality is also greatly enhanced by the wide range of sensations a phantom limb can experience.

Their vivid sensory qualities and precise location in space make the limbs seem so lifelike that a patient may even attempt to get off a bed onto a phantom foot or surprisingly enough lift a glass with a phantom hand. The phantom at times seems more substantial than an actual limb, particularly if it hurts.

Of all the feelings in phantom limbs, pain is the most frightening and disturbing. It is often sensed as burning, cramping or shooting, and may vary from being occasional and mild to continuous and severe. A usual complaint is that a hand is clenched, fingers bent over the thumb and digging into the palm, so that the whole hand is tired and achy. In the leg the discomfort may be felt as a cramp in the calf. Many patients report that their toes feel as if they are being seared by a red-hot poker.

A phantom arm, in most cases, hangs down at the side when the person sits or stands, but it moves in perfect coordination with other limbs during walking. Strangely enough, it behaves like a normal limb. Similarly, a phantom leg bends when its body sits. It becomes upright during standing and stretches out when the person lies down.

The eerie reality of phantoms is often strengthened by sensations that mimic feelings in the limb before amputation. The sense of reality is also strengthened by the wide range of sensations a phantom limb can have. Warmth, cold, and pressure are some of the common experiences. The patient may also feel as if the limb is being tickled or is sweaty or prickly.

A person may sense a painful ulcer or bunion that had been on a foot or even a tight ring that had been on a finger. Such patients are not merely remembering sensations but are feeling them with the full intensity and detail of an ongoing experience. Even when the foot is felt to be dangling in the air several inches beneath the stump and unconnected to the leg, it is still experienced as part of the body and it moves appropriately with the other limbs and with the torso. The reality of the phantom is also enhanced by wearing an artificial arm or leg. The phantom usually fills the prosthesis as a hand fits a glove.

Paraplegics, persons who have had a complete break of the spinal cord and have no control over their body below the fracture, also experience the phantom limb. After an accident the phantom limb may appear disconnected from the real body. The paraplegic may even experience the limbs in unusual positions although the visible limbs are stretched out on the road.

The many explanations for phantom limbs and their associated pain are always insufficient. Clearly, the source of phantom limbs is more complex than any of the theories suggest. There simply do not exist any proposed hypotheses that explain away all of the enigmas surrounding the phantom limb phenomenon. The problem essentially boils down to the level of consciousness of the researchers who may observe complex phenomena with muddled or chaotic solutions.

The reason for the failure of science to arrive at conclusive decisions and explanations is the scientists' obstinate and unyielding refusal to alter their consciousness.

Scientists cling to the belief that understanding existence and its manifestations lies in researching the processes and laws of nature. However, what is omitted from the research is the "why" of creation and the factors that cause it to operate in that orderly a fashion. This is true of all research, whether it concerns the big bang, dinosaurs, phantom limbs or stress.

To ignore the issue of causality and the purpose *behind* each cause and effect leaves the field of physics in an incomplete state.

I am certain that as we probe nature more deeply, we will uncover a whole new era in physics and medicine, one more basic and more beautiful. This sentiment has already been voiced by John Wheeler, the famous astrophysicist, who wrote, "Some day a door will surely open and expose the glittering central mechanism of the world in its beauty and simplicity. Toward the arrival of that day, no development holds out more hope than the para-dox[340] of gravitational collapse."[341]

The path to this new age of science, which lies beyond the boundaries set by our rational mind (the Dark-Lord con-sciousness) where limits of the physical world cease to exist, is provided by the Zohar. Rabbi Shimon bar Yohai, in his *Book of Splendor*, realized that in order to face the unknowable — and heaven knows how many of those events beset our daily lives — it would be necessary to discover the *cause* of these events, an undertaking that presents a difficulty with which contemporary physics cannot, and has no desire to cope.

It is precisely this encounter with the unknowable that some scientists are declaring forever sealed and beyond the domain of intellectual inquiry. Yet ancient Kabbalists held the key, as the following Zohar will indicate.

> Another reason why the body should be buried on the same day is that when the soul departs from the body it cannot enter the other world until it is invested with another body formed of light. So Elijah had two bodies, one in which he appeared on earth, and one in which he appeared among celestial angels.
>
> So long as the body remains unburied the soul suffers pain and an unclean spirit rests upon the body. Therefore, the body should not be kept over-night, because by night the unclean spirit spreads over the earth, seeking for a body without a soul to defile it.[342]

What seems to emerge from the Zohar is a phenomenon

best described as worlds, entities, or universes that are parallel and interrelated, yet independent. We might crudely compare this phenomenal concept to our present day computer systems which may include many varied programs within their software.

By the path of Kabbalah, we can gain an insight into the *whys* of the entire spectrum of the body where the scientist has found barriers he is still unable to penetrate. The knowledge of revealment, Kabbalistic knowledge, provides explanations for the movements of human and bodily activity. We thus have taken a giant step forward in bridging the gap and providing the necessary link between celestial, metaphysical and corporeal, terrestrial entities.

What the previously mentioned Zohar reveals for us is a duality that exists within the human body — one that we are all familiar with, and another that can be revealed to those of an elevated consciousness such as "Elijah" who appeared among celestial angels in that other body.

With this understanding, the problems created by the "phantom limb" become very real. All attempts to manipulate and sever the pain channels of the physical body will be of no avail. We cannot, with physical surgical procedures, alter the effect that the metaphysical, non-perceived second body has upon the human senses. This additional body recognizes and experiences the pain and trauma of being deprived access into the physical plane due to the severance of the physical limb.

Rather than choose the negative approach to the problems of the phantom limb sufferer — severing nerves and other methods with the usual trial and error game plan — let us concentrate on and accentuate the positive approach of the Kabbalists: restoring the lost limb.[343] For the present, this idea, that man can control his physical environment, and even his own body is unthinkable. The past two thousand years of lack of control have left an indelible mark upon the consciousness of man.

The vast majority of traditional scientists, clergy and laymen could not, nor will they, entertain for a moment the idea that the human mind can influence the phenomenon of physical reality. Yet Scriptures ask us to accept without question that consciousness can enable certain individuals to transcend the laws of physics. Who, or what are we to believe?

Quantum theory affirms that human intervention influences the structure of physical reality. The revelation of the Zohar, with its careful scrutiny of the physical and metaphysical anatomy of the individual, allows us to learn exactly what exists in the realm of the galaxy and quantum, as well as in the realm of undiscovered celestial and terrestrial objects. The Zohar[344] states:

> Upon man *rests* the entire movement and strings of the universe. For there is not a member in the *human* body that does not have its counterpart in the universe as a whole. For as man's body is divided and subdivided into sections and all are poised upon levels of different magnetic fields and intelligence, by which each react and interact with the other so as to form one organism although remaining independent, so is the entire universe based upon parallel and different levels by which each section, each segment of the universe is related and interrelated with the other.

Two remarkable statements emerge from the Zohar. Man, by Kabbalistic standards, is the determining producer and director of movement in this universe. Furthermore, man is featured as a carbon copy of everything, both in the celestial and terrestrial realm of our universe. Both declarations tend to sound incredible in light of man's latest technology, where the only place man has walked beyond the earth is the moon.

The pure scientist may shake his head in despair at the previous Zoharic statement, but the Zohar makes it clear: Man's consciousness is an inherent dynamism. This impels the Zoharic conclusion that the whole of the cosmos consists of consciousness and consequently is subject to man's consciousness.[345] To attach the idea of consciousness to the cosmos is what I consider the most daring of all Zoharic declarations. This revelation is indeed overwhelming.

Consequently, for the Kabbalist to consider the awesome power inherent within man capable of restoring limbs is not considered so far-out. It is our inability to define and recognize the various entities of consciousness and intelligence at the subatomic or celestial levels that bars us from initiating what most of us consider a miracle.

Rabbi Shimon bar Yoḥai, who achieved an extremely high degree of an altered state of consciousness, found no difficulty in his total control over every aspect of our universe.[346]

To further confuse this issue of mind power control and consciousness, the famous 20th century Danish physicist Neils Bohr said, "If you don't see it, it isn't there." But surely the world out there exists whether or not we are looking at it. The chair upon which I am sitting may have disappeared subatomically, but I am not likely to fall to the floor.

The answer lies in the consciousness of the mind. The mind element appears to be essential to our observation of the real, metaphysical world. In other words, because we have decided that we are seated on a chair, the physical chair responds to *our* consciousness that a chair exists.

The real problem that Einstein had with this theory was that, while the theory was absolutely correct, it just didn't have any relevance to his actual life. If, for example, he left his keys at home when he went to the classroom, he could not enter his house when he returned. Now, according to his theory, all he had to do was not allow the existence of the door to enter his consciousness.

To accomplish this would require an altered state of consciousness. There is no question that this sort of thinking about the physical, illusionary world is new to the Western mind, especially to the layman.

However, we must refer to it in order to illustrate how unfamiliar we are with this physical world. Touching upon a more serious note, we must ask of ourselves, if the physicists, Neils Bohr and his colleagues, are indeed correct in their conclusions concerning reality, then why can't a person with cancer send signals along nerves to enhance defenses and make the body fight more aggressively against disease? Why can't the patient deal with illness the same way the physicist claims we can relate to a chair? "If you don't see it, it isn't there."

By the same reasoning, why can't our mind consciousness restore a phantom limb, kidney or any part of our body by the same consciousness of "If you do see it, then it is there." The idea of restoring life and certainly limbs has already been mentioned in Scriptures.[347] The sages of the Mishnah were known to resurrect people from the dead.

Let us now refer to the Zoharic text[348] where the resurrection and restoration of limbs are specifically dealt with.

> Come and see. When they shall arise from the
> dust at the time of the resurrection of the dead, as
> they entered into the grave, so shall they rise. If
> they were lame or blind when they died, then
> they shall rise as lame and blind, in the exact
> physical body so that it shall not be said that it
> was someone else who was brought back to life.
> And afterwards the Lord shall heal them. And all
> shall be complete and perfect. And then the entire
> world shall emerge complete in every aspect. And
> then "in that day the Lord and his vessel shall be
> one."[349]

Rabbi Ashlag in his introduction to his commentary, the
"Ladder Interpretation" raises some very interesting questions on
the Zohar just mentioned. Why is it necessary that the dead be
brought back to life with their deformities that existed in their
prior lifetime? What does the Zohar imply when it declares "so
that it shall not be said that it was someone else who was brought
back to life?" Why is the Zohar so concerned as to what others
might think at the time of the resurrection? Who might think?

Furthermore, why must the Lord await the appearance of
these deformed corpses before He can heal them? Additionally
the statement concerning the entire world and its final completion in every aspect seems to depend first upon the healing of
those resurrected. Why is this so?

A thorough and complete explanation to this very confusing Zohar will depend on our previously mentioned Zohar concerning the two bodies of Elijah, the prophet. Let us therefore
explore the interpretation of Rabbi Ashlag[350] and decidedly we

shall come to some startling revelations concerning the phantom limbs.

> Self reflection reveals to us our imperfections and lowly position. Yet how is this possible seeing that we have been created by the Lord whose perfect agency must necessarily produce perfect works? However, according to what we have just explained, it should now be perfectly understood that the body that we possess, with all its insignificant components and categories is *not* really our *true* body; that is to say, the eternal one that is completely perfect, is to be found already existing in the "Blessed Endless" in the aspect of Phase One (where all was eternally perfect).[351]

> It is there that it receives its perfect form from that which will ultimately come about in Phase Three,[352] namely "receiving in the form of imparting," which is a state that is "similar in form"[353] to the "Blessed Endless." Therefore it is Phase One that requires that Phase Two[354] contain the "shell" (*Klippah*) of that body that we possess in its despicable and imperfect form — namely the "will to receive for oneself alone," which is a force that brings separation from the "Blessed Endless."

> It is given to us in Phase Two so that we should correct it so that it should be possible for us to receive our *eternal* body in Phase Three. We should not have any complaints at all about that. Our work cannot be conceived of as happening only in this perishable body. We should constant-

ly be located, even in Phase Two, in that degree of perfection that is *fitting* and *appropriate* for the perfect Creator who created us.

This body is no blemish to us in any way for it will perish and disappear. It has only been prepared for us for the amount of time that it is necessary for us to eliminate it and so receive our eternal form.

What clearly emerges from the idea presented by Rabbi Ashlag is that we do in fact possess two bodies. The illusionary, unreal one, has been placed with our soul and eternal body for the express purpose of providing us with an opportunity for "restriction" and the *removal* of Bread of Shame, the *removal* of the Dark Lord's consciousness of "desire to receive for oneself alone," the energy fuel of the illusionary body.

This is what the religionist refers to as "service for the Lord." In actuality the service and effort are for *mankind's* benefit and not for the Lord's. He neither needs nor requires our services. I'm certain that the Lord can manage very well without the support and assistance that we believe benefits the Lord with our so-called service. Our efforts must be directed toward the removal of the illusionary Satanic influence of ego and our selfish desires, and return to the elevated state of consciousness of a desire to receive for the sake of sharing.

One of the significant methods by which we can arrive at our *Tikune* (correction) is to negate each and every physical or physically-related pleasure, whether it be the compliment of a friend which may stimulate our ego or the apple that satisfies our physical body of illusion. However, in an elevated state of consciousness we accept the apple with the *awareness* that the

Creator created the apple for the express purpose of benefitting mankind. At that moment, we are directing our consciousness to accept the apple for the pleasure of consummating the Creator's "Thought of Creation" which is to impart His beneficence.

Through this procedure and process, we fuel our other body, the eternal one which is similar but is an extension of the Lord. We have created a similarity and affinity with the eternal body and the Creator Whose consciousness is to "share." Lacking fuel and sustenance, the illusionary body loses its state of consciousness and thus permits the spiritual growth of the eternal body.

By means of our work and service at negating[355] this "desire to receive for oneself alone" we succeed in attaining all the beautiful levels that are in the souls which are termed Crude Spirit, Spirit, Soul, Living and Oneness. Attaining the greatest possible spiritual perfection of a "desire to receive for the sake of sharing" it is then possible for the unreal body to be brought to life again with its extensive desire to receive. This body will no longer be in a position to harm us by separating us from close attachment to the Lightforce.

On the contrary, we will take control of it, and give it the form of "imparting." But as long as we have not yet removed the "self indulgence of desire to receive," it will be impossible to *direct* it along the desired middle way.[356]

Rabbi Ashlag leads us to the conclusion that when the Zohar speaks of the resurrection of the body, it does not exclusively refer to the dead. The process of resurrection has been a continuous process from the very beginning of Creation. This refers to the unreal body, which is the consciousness of the extensive "will to receive for the self alone" — without any limits or restrictions — as it developed in Phase Two within the chariots of the World of Cleanliness[357] before we succeeded in purifying it through Kabbalah and Precepts. Thus, we are referring to the unreal body in its extreme state of all its infirmities.

The infirmities are the direct result of our succumbing to the dominant consciousness of Satan and his "desire to receive for the self alone." This was a necessary requirement to achieve *Tikune*. For we now had the opportunity to rise to the challenge of transforming this deadly consciousness by channeling it towards a consciousness of imparting. Then, and only then, it and the resultant deformities will be *healed*.[358]

The Zohar states that the reason for the resurrection is so that "they" should not say that, "he is another," meaning that he is in a different form than he was in Phase One, within the "Thought of Creation." For in Phase One, the extensive and supreme "desire to receive" was ready to receive *all* the good that was in the Thought of Creation. In the meantime (Phase Two), the body was given over to the "shells" (*Klippot*) for the opportunity of purification.

> In the final event [ultimately] it is impossible that it remain "another body," for if its proportions were actually reduced in any way, it *would* then be like a completely different body. And then it would not be at all suitable to receive any of the good that is contained in the Thought of Creation as it was receiving there in Phase One.[359]

This remarkable interpretation clears up the misconception that any part of our body "can be another," namely, that our bodies might remain eternally deformed or without limbs. Furthermore, that it is within *our* power and consciousness to restore these missing or deformed limbs to their prior state of Phase One where they were complete and whole. In addition, the cause of these deformities lies in *our own* negative (deformed) states of consciousness, which, when transformed, will restore these missing and deformed limbs to their prior state of perfection.

The reason for these so-called miracles never making their appearance has been directly linked to our inability to heal ourselves from one state of consciousness — desire for the self alone — to the consciousness of imparting. However, states the Ari and the Zohar, all this is possible in our Age of Aquarius. The folklore abounds with stories surrounding the Hasidic masters[360] who were capable of healing deformities and restoring limbs.

The intent of this section of my work is to awaken the consciousness within us that in our times these miracles are possible. However, by the same token, we cannot achieve these

miracles if we remain stubborn as skeptics and refuse to try it out. After all, can we truly afford the luxury of being a skeptic when at stake is the possibility for self-healing of all disabilities and illnesses?

With the foregoing, we have achieved a breakthrough in comprehending the entire mystery surrounding phantom limbs. To start with, persons who have lost an arm or leg perceive the limb as though it is still there because it is and always will be present, as long as the individual is physically alive. Additionally, the illusionary arm feels the excruciating pain, because, as stated in the Zohar, "we shall not say that it was someone else," meaning that because of the absence of the physical arm there is no possibility to change from being "another body," the ultimate purpose of being like the real arm.

The metaphysical pain, the consciousness of failing to remove the non-spiritual consciousness of the Dark Lord ultimately becomes physically manifested. Thus, the areas where the patient has not fulfilled the *Tikune* process, the distorted, deformed or missing limb suffers the distress of not returning to the level of spirituality that the real arm experiences and enjoys. The phantom feels dissociated from the real body.

A paraplegic — one who has fractures in the spinal cord and therefore has no feeling or control over the body below the break — may often have phantom legs and other phantom body parts. The paraplegic may feel that the legs that are unseen are raised above the head, while the legs that are seen are lying flat.

Sometimes, these same paraplegics complain that their legs are in continuous motion producing painful fatigue despite the patients' legs lying in a paralysis state. Here again, the reason for tiredness lies in the fact that the real body connected to the

Lightforce is not affected by the immobility of the lost, phantom leg. There is no chaos within the *real* body. Movement and sensation are features that the real body never loses. Consequently, the resulting fatigue is constantly present if the mind of the patient is in a state of moving the leg.

Unfortunately, the conventional explanation given for phantom limbs and their pain is associated with the remaining nerves in the stump, or any other internal organ which continues to generate impulses. Consequently, the treatment recommended is to halt these sensory transmissions. From a Kabbalistic perspective, we are treating this matter with an analgesic, because the pain will never cease even if we completely anesthetize the body to a vegetable state. The real body is not the illusionary "other body" of the patient. That "other body" will constantly remain influenced and affected by the real body to abandon its satanic-rational consciousness of the "desire to receive for oneself alone," the ultimate goal, so that it not remain the "other body."

The fact is that the medical approaches may provide relief for months or even years. However, the pain usually returns. Moreover, none of these procedures abolishes the phantom limb itself. Therefore, neuronal activity cannot by itself account for either the phenomenon of the phantom limb or for the suffering. Alterations or surgical therapy cannot by themselves account for phantoms and their pain.

The Zohar and the works of Rabbi Isaac Luria and Rabbi Ashlag lead us to conclude that, with proper consciousness and meditation, lost limbs or deformities *can* and *will* be restored in this Age of Aquarius; far-out for too many of us to understand, and least of all, to accept.

Nevertheless, new medical advances have simply been out

of touch with reality. The latest reports indicate that for every step forward in medical research, science takes giant steps backwards. The increase of illness among the world's population have reached epidemic proportions.

Before closing this chapter, I feel it important to extend this newly expressed phenomenon to the Judeo-Christian position on the Resurrection of the Dead. The idea of resurrection is commonly linked to the coming of the Messiah when all dead corpses, worthy of resurrection, shall rise again.

However, following the interpretation by Rabbi Ashlag that the concept of resurrection also applies to those yet alive but have no limbs, organs or suffer paralysis, the following Zohar expresses some very significant points of interest. The Zohar[361] throws light on the stages leading up to and including the coming of the Messiah.

> The only difference between the world as we see and observe it today and the Age of Aquarius is *Shiabud Malkhut* [slavery to *Malkhut* — knuckling under the yoke of the desire to receive for oneself alone]. And the only difference between the world as we see it and observe it today and the period of the Resurrection of the Dead is the human cleansing process and acquiring knowledge that will have occurred. Rabbi Nahman said: The difference will be reflected in an extended life span.
>
> Rabbi Joseph said: Is the Age of Aquarius and Resurrection of the Dead not one and the same? He said to him: No! For we have learned that the Holy Temple precedes the ingathering of the

exiles. The ingathering of the exiles precedes the Resurrection of the Dead, and the Resurrection of the Dead is the final and last stage. Where is this indicated in Scriptures? The Lord builds Jerusalem: he gathers together the exiles of Israel. He heals the brokenhearted and binds up their wounds.[362] 'Heals the broken hearted' refers to the Resurrection.

The ingathering of the exiles will precede the Resurrection by forty years. What will transpire during these forty years? Said Rabbi Kahana in the name of Rabbi Beruka. "During this period between the ingathering of the exiles and Resurrection, many difficulties and wars shall descend on Israel and praiseworthy for those who shall survive."

What seems to emerge from the preceding Zohar is the idea that in the Age of Aquarius, humankind will begin to notice the futility of excess desires for oneself alone and that in the period of Resurrection, mankind will begin to observe the benefits of cleansing "the other body" and acquire knowledge to which the layman never had access.

This Zohar corresponds to the Zohar mentioned previously, that with proper cleansing and *knowledge*, mankind shall be the forerunner and minister for the phenomenon of Resurrection. Upon man and his consciousness rests the notion of Resurrection. Whether this enigma relates to the restoration of a limb or the resurrection of the dead, we are not to wait for these joyous moments to descend upon us by the graciousness of the Divine. Man possesses the ability to achieve the elevated states of consciousness to restore limbs and resurrect the dead. The

Talmud is replete with accounts of reviving the dead[363] by the sages of the Tannaic[364] period, including, of course, the Prophet Ezekiel[365].

Another interesting point to take note of is the statement of the Zohar that the Holy Temple precedes the ingathering of the exiles. This event has in effect already taken place as noted in the Zohar.[366] In addition, the Zohar states: "the ingathering of the exiles will precede the Resurrection by forty years." This ingathering is in process of becoming a reality. Howard M. Sacher, professor of History and consultant and lecturer on Middle Eastern affairs describes the ingathering in his book, *A History of Israel*:[367]

> In the eighteen months following the Declaration of Independence 340,000 Jews arrived in Israel. During the [British] mandate the rate of immigration had averaged 18,000 *a year*.... During the first three years of statehood the average reached 18,000 *a month* and in some months the figure exceeded 30,000. Between May 15, 1948 and June 30, 1957 the Jewish population of the country doubled. No influx like it had been witnessed in modern times. It was an "open door" from which older and vastly wealthier nations would have recoiled in dismay.

* * *

> The demographic impact of the immigration was profound. Fully 7 percent of the entire Diaspora arrived in Israel beween 1948 and 1953 alone. The numbers of Jewish inhabitants accordingly rose from 6 percent of world Jewry at the founding of

the state to 13 percent by the end of 1953. During its initial four and a half years Israel's population doubled. By the end of 1956 its population had nearly tripled, reaching 1,667,000.

To carry the story of the immigration to a further period the following is reported in *The American Jewish Year Book* for 1991 (prepared by the American Jewish Committee):

The Year 1989 saw the largest immigration of Soviet Jews since the 1920's. Whereas the year 1988 about 20,000 had left, according to HIAS, 70,508 Jews left in 1989 of whom 17% went to Israel.... However, owing to a change in U.S. Policy, by December, 41 percent of the emigres went to Israel. In September, Israeli Prime Minister Yitzhak Shamir predicted that a million Soviet Jews would emigrate and argued that they should come primarily to Israel.

By no coincidence, during this period which ended with his passing in 1955, Rabbi Ashlag completed all of his works necessary to enlighten all of humankind in preparation for our cleansing which would be required for the Resurrection, as stated in the Zohar.

Rabbi Ashlag revolutionized the entire structure of physics. When he completed his first work in 1920, he had already set into motion all of the revolutionary and weird ideas that were subsequently to emerge in the world of physics. Unfortunately, science paid far more attention to the science of physics than the true reality of metaphysics to which Rabbi Ashlag had applied himself. He combined the two realities and reconciled each with the other. Unfortunately, physicists still cling to the world of uncertainty, refusing to concede the existence of another reality.

As the universe consists of two realities, so does our corporeal bodies. With a thorough understanding of both, which can only come about by and with Kabbalistic studies, science will be worthy of "observing a beautiful, simple world of existence out there."368

Now let us turn to another section of this Zohar:369

Said Rabbi Yehudah in the name of Rav: The Lord shall rejoice in that period with the righteous to endow upon them the [quantum] knowledge of the *Shekhinah*. And *everyone* will participate in that joyous event as it is written: the Lord shall rejoice in his actions.370 Said Rabbi Yehudah: The righteous in that period will create the world and resurrect the dead.

Said Rabbi Yosi: Did we not learn that, "there is nothing new under the sun."371 Answered Rabbi Yehudah: Come and hear. As long as the wicked dominate in the world, and create strife, the entire world remains unstable and in chaos. However, when the righteous control, then the entire world is stable and they will in the future resurrect the dead as we have already discussed in Scriptures: "Old men and old women shall yet again dwell in the streets of Jerusalem, and every man with his staff in his hand for every age,"372 as is written before.373

In that time, the righteous shall acquire complete

knowledge, as Rabbi Yosi said: "In those days that
the Lord shall rejoice in his works, the righteous
shall acquire the Lightforce in their hearts, and
wisdom shall increase in their hearts as if they see
it with their eyes."

The greatest problem as I see it, is the difficulty of convincing mankind of their capability to control their own lives, even to
the extent of regaining their health and restoring missing limbs.
This, together with scientific conclusions that are presently incomprehensible, presents a picture of confusion. For the most part people are resigned to deal with their chaos on a day to day basis.

Little do we realize that as Murphy's law implies, "If anything can go wrong, it will." Gaps or cracks in our reasoning are
easily filled or replaced by the negative world of the Dark Lord.
Complacency and feelings of shallow security are false guarantees
that our problems will fade away.

However, as the Zohar states, in this Age of Aquarius all
of mankind shall be subject to an information revolution. We
shall no longer be content with some fast, unreal and superficial
reasoning or solutions. The consciousness of the entire world has
been elevated.

Because of the Aquarian Age sphere of influence, a new
vision of reality, a fundamental change in our perceptions and
values, is already pervading the entire planet. Man has begun to
challenge the external influences of the media and politicians. No
longer is man content to be persuaded by what others are doing
out there. We're beginning to raise questions that were never
thought of in the past.

Man is once again being called upon to take hold of the

reins of a galloping, runaway universe. The violent and reckless behavior presently occurring demands that the responsibility for our destiny return to the people with adequate sensible government.

In conclusion, let us remember that, in truth, there is nothing out there but consciousness. We shall gradually realize that the physical world out there is illusionary, a fact already confirmed by scientists. In addition, we shall abandon the rational consciousness for what it represents, an agent of the Dark Lord.

It is a complicated mess out there. Instead of a complete quantum view of the external world we allow the Dark Lord to occupy its myriad of passageways. We, thus direct the mechanical mind towards the Dark Lord's goal of ultimate chaos and uncertainty.

In essence, we never operate with a "full deck." The reason is that, unfortunately, we succumb to the influence of the Dark Lord. However, we do have the good fortune of witnessing the Age of Aquarius in our time. And therefore have access into the quantum information about the inside and outside worlds of existence. As stated in Scripture: "One day they will no longer teach every man his brother saying, know the Lord, for they shall all *know* me, from the youngest to the oldest of them."[374]

As with new ideas, they are usually rejected outright. However, in the absence of new, dramatic developments, the people of the world will quickly adjust to these new declarations of the Kabbalah. So when we even consider an outrageous idea such as the restoration of a limb or part of the body, in this Age of Aquarius the hunger for new knowledge will far outweigh the conservative viewpoints that have always dominated the minds of humankind.

An illustration of what we may expect in the way of out of the ordinary events in this Age of Aquarius is clearly stated by the Ari, Rabbi Isaac Luria, in his work entitled the *Gates of the Holy Spirit.*[375]

Let us therefore return to the incredible notion presented by the Ari that in our Age of Aquarius, missing limbs and other parts of the physical body can and will be restored to their former state of existence. The first question that must be raised is, why doesn't a severed arm return to its previous condition? The DNA, the blueprint and origin of our physical makeup, has not disappeared. If, after cutting our hair or nails, the hair and nails continue to grow, why not the bone structure?

Why have we accepted the aging and degeneration process as part of human existence? The singular proof of its existence seems to be that all around us we *see* its effects and never do see a reversal of the aging process. However, let us remember that "what the eye does not see is not proof that it does not exist."

Furthermore, the "phantom hand" phenomenon remains just that, a phenomenon. When someone has lost an arm, he or she experiences the entire arm as still attached to their body. On many occasions, they feel a sensation of "itching" and react as any other person by reaching out and scratching the arm. However, the eye does not see the arm where it should be.

What the Ari offers in this Age of Aquarius is the idea that miracles are out there just waiting to be revealed. The paranormal is reality whereas the seeable may indeed exist as an illusion. So too with miracles (like the splitting of the Red Sea) that have become accepted phenomena of a supernatural event.

At first glance, the notion presented by the Ari certainly seems far out. But those rejecting outright the idea of restoring a lost limb had better expand their limited awareness. A skeptic is not usually the one who has researched the matter and laid bare the facts to arrive at skepticism.

I realize that this concept requires a transformation of our accepted thinking process. However, what I am proposing from a Zoharic perspective is nothing short of a consciousness revolution. There are no shortcuts to the attainment of a state of fulfillment. However, these objectives are reachable in our time, in this Age of Aquarius.

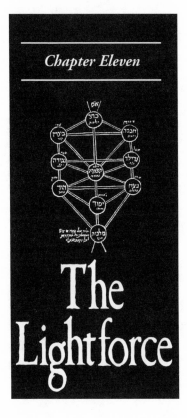

Chapter Eleven

The Lightforce

And the Lord said,
Let there be Light:
And there was Light.
And the Lord saw the
Light, that it was good:
And the Lord divided the
Light from the darkness.
And the Lord called the
Light Day, and the dark-
ness He called Night.
And there was evening
and there was morning,
one day.

Genesis 1:3-5

THERE ARE MANY QUESTIONS THAT SCIENCE CANNOT confidently answer on the basis of theory and experiment. The scientist can only speculate as can we all. If not science, where then do we begin our investigation into the question of why and how did life and the universe originate? Our initial exposure to this question is through the Biblical account of Genesis.

However, the Biblical version of the creation of the universe is vague concerning what exactly transpired. The Zohar repeatedly states that the entire Bible is a cosmic code. Creation is, for the uninitiated reader, decidedly abstruse. Rashi, the greatest commentator of all time, taught that a strict chronology of Creation was not the purpose of Scripture. No less an authority than Maimonides declared: "The account given in Scripture of the Creation is not, as is generally believed, intended to be in all its parts literal."

In face of the great diversity of opinion and views as to the mode of Creation, there is nothing inherently anti-bible in the theory of evolution of forms of existence from the simple to the complex, and from the highest to the lowest. Each stage is not a product of chance, but is an act of Divine consciousness that has no desire other than to share.[376]

Behind the orderly development of the universe there must be a cause, at once *controlling* and *permeating* the process. Allowing for all the evidence in favor of interpreting existence in terms of the doctrine of evolution, there still remain significant factors yet to be explained, e.g., the origin of our universe, the meaning of light, etc. For each of these, we must turn to the Creative Omnipotence of the Original Spirit and the interpretation given by the Zohar.

Evolution is conceivable only as the activity of a Creative Consciousness for the purpose of making the Thought of Creation[377] a physical reality by means of precise universal laws reaching its climax in man endowed with the realization of manifesting the original thought of the Creator. In other words, the ultimate goal of creation was man — last in manifestation, first in thought.[378]

There exists within man a passion for comprehension. More so than ever in history, the Age of Aquarius has incited the thirst for simplicity and inspired a need to know. Fifty years ago science seemed to be on the road to clear cut answers to ancient questions. But it proved to be more complicated than that. Today a physicist is no closer to the enigmatic phenomena that pervade our universe than he was then. In fact science admits that our conception of material reality today is more wavering and uncertain than it has been for a long time.

We know a great many interesting details, learn new ones every week. But to construct a clear, easily comprehensible picture with which all physicists would agree, is simply impossible. At present, Physics stands at a grave crisis of ideas. In the face of this crisis, many scientists maintain that no objective picture of reality is possible.

Enter the Zohar and its interpretation of the Lightforce. The first day of Creation mentions the concept of Light. For mankind, the notion of natural light is normally associated with the sun and its sunlight. However, closely examining the Biblical description of the first account of Creation,[379] the appearance of the sun followed during the fourth day of Creation. An obvious question that must be raised at this time is, just what does the Bible refer to when it states: "And the Lord said, let there be Light?"

Furthermore, what is the intention of Scripture when it states: "And the Lord saw the Light, that it was *good*?" Additionally, the verse mentions that the Lord said: "Let there be Light, and there was Light." What does this imply? Does it indicate that by the Lord's conscious thought to have light it became a reality, that light, in fact, became a living entity? Where did this light emerge from? And more importantly, what is the essence and substance of the Light considered in this most important section of the entire Biblical text?

"LIGHT, AND THERE WAS LIGHT."[380] These words imply that there had already been light. The Hebrew word for light, *Or* contains within itself a deep and hidden significance. [The Hebrew letter *Yud* had previously diminished the light to the ethereal level known by the code name *Avir* ("air or ether," *aleph vav yud resh*). Hence the difference between the Hebrew word for light, *Or* (*alef vav resh*) and the light's concealment known as *Avir* is that the Hebrew letter *Yud* is inserted in the word *Or* to become *Avir*].

The expansive force proceeding from the hidden recesses of the secret supernal ether opened a path and produced from itself the renewed revealment of the *En Sof*[81] the Endless Light. When this expanded, that which was left of the mysterious *Avir* (*alef vav yud resh*) was found to be *Or* (*alef vav resh*). When the first point [the letter *Yud*[82] having pierced the *Avir*, the ethereal light complex] had developed from it [*Avir*], It [Light of the Endless] showed itself upon it, touching and yet not touching it.

When It [Light of the Endless] further expanded, it emerged into being, and thus was Light (*alef vav resh*) left from ether (*alef vav yud resh*) and this is what we mean by saying that it "had been" previously; and so it remained. It went up and was stored away, and there was left of it one dot, which continually approaches by invisible paths the other point, touching and yet not touching, illuminating it in the manner of the first point from which it issued.

Therefore, the whole is linked together, and it illumines both one and the other. When it ascends, all ascend and are attached to it, and it reaches the place of *En Sof*, where it is stored

away, and all becomes one. This dot of the word
Avir is Light.[383]

To the uninitiated reader, the foregoing Zohar may be
more confusing concerning the subject under consideration,
namely the Light, than if no mention of the Zohar were made.
However, for the purpose of this volume, the reader will become
familiar with the minimal degree of needed information to comprehend the idea of Light. A full explanation of this apparently
abstruse Zohar has already been provided by Rabbi Ashlag in the
original text of this section in the Zohar.

What does seem to emerge from the Zohar is that light,
as we know it, is not the essence of Light, but is rather the
essence enclothed in another form, and thus becomes revealed.
This might be compared to the body and soul of man, where the
internal force of the soul, the Light of the Lord, becomes
enclothed in a corporeal body and thus becomes a noticeable and
dominant force. The body, as all other corporeal, material entities, has no life force of its own. When the life or light force
leaves, the material fades away and decays.

The sun, created on the fourth day was another extension
of the process of evolution. The Lightforce of *En Sof,* in whatever
form it makes its appearance does not undergo any changes. The
Light always remains within the Kabbalistic doctrine of *Yesh Me
Yesh,* existence from existence.[384] The only changes that the
Lightforce *seems* to undergo is when the Light becomes revealed
in an infinite array of manifestations making it appear as if trans-
formations take place within the Lightforce.

The body consciousness of man, the five satanic senses, is
limited to grasping the physical reality. When man is asleep, the
body-consciousness' control over the soul comes to an end.

Unlike the body, the soul is not subject to the space-time paradigm of past, present and future. The soul has access to the quantum consciousness, where past, present and future exist in a single all-inclusive multidimensional place. Total control by the soul over the environment, over the future, is indeed possible.

Why? Because the soul is a "part of the Lord," an extension of the Endless Light.[385] The question that may be asked at this time is how do we comprehend and accept the idea that the all-inclusive Light of the Endless can adjust to the varied manifestations experienced in our mundane world? The awesome power of the Lightforce should not be contained or restricted by the demands placed upon it by the vessel or recipient.[386]

Inasmuch as the original thought of Creation by the Lord or Creator was to "share,"[387] the demands or requests by the recipient must be acknowledged and honored by the Lightforce. Why? The answer is that a "desire to share" depends on the willingness of the vessel to accept the beneficence, for without the vessel's consent, coercing the vessel to accept against the vessel's will, cannot be considered "sharing," hence the spiritual concept of "no coercion in spirituality."

The reason for the "distinction of a multitude of manifestations," answers the Zohar, "is due solely and primarily to our way of perceiving the world, a result of the perception of the Lightforce by finite, created beings."[388] The Innermost Being of the Divinity (*En Sof*), and the Lightforce as an extension of the Deity, motivated and initiated the creation of the vessel(s) — soul, and the *Sfirot* — vessels which would ultimately enclothe It and would benefit from Its beneficence.

The motivating Thought of Creation, which was to impart beneficence to man through the Desire to Receive, influenced the

emergence of the multiform characteristic of the Light, which could fill and nourish these vessels with an infinite quantity of abundance. In other words, the Lightforce, in its infinite Desire to Impart, required and caused the manifestation of a correspondingly infinite number of souls which would desire this beneficence.

Thus this first and primary world, the state of *En Sof* (the infinite) is given this symbolic name in accordance with the endless variety of degree of receiving that took place within the union of the Lightforce with the Kingdom (*Malkhut*) of the *En Sof.* In all this it should be remembered that the Divine Light remained a total unity, as noted in the passage, "I am the Lord, I do not change."[389]

The notion that the Lightforce is composed of a quantum nature has already been established by 20th century physicists. An inferometer, a device that splits and then recombines beams of light, holds a venerable place in the history of experimental physics. It was invented more than a century ago by the renowned physicist, Albert Michelson, who together with noted chemist Edward Morley, found that the orbital motion of Earth has *no* effect on the speed of light, despite Einstein's theory that the "speed of light" is limited to a speed of 286,000 miles per second.

That discovery paved the way for Albert Einstein and his theory that the speed of light is *constant* regardless of whether the observer is departing from the light or approaching it. The key point at this time is that physicists have found that nothing in the laws of physics contradicts the notion that light has no speed.

Some day someone will do what fiction characters do now: speed through hyperspace to a galactic outpost traveling faster than the speed of light. At present, scientists have come to the conclusion that if we could travel at the speed of light, time would actually proceed into the past.

Mathematical formulae agree with the scriptural verse[390] that suggests two-way time travel. However, for the most part, the paradoxical consequences of "no speed of light," keep it within the framework of science fiction.[391]

The basic problem facing the physicist mathematician is that this phenomenon challenges our most rigid laws of science and principles of logic. Once we travel faster than the speed of light, then we must consider the possibility of stumbling upon the Fountain of Youth. We reverse the steady pattern of time passing into the past and, thus, eliminate the reality that people must grow old.

This discrepancy is resolved when we accept the Zoharic contention of a reality of two parallel universes. The spiritual body is connected with the Lightforce, the Tree of Life universe. The closer we get to the speed of light, the slower our watch will run. If we could reach the speed of light, time would stop altogether. Earthly time has been well documented as elastic time or time dilation.

The problem of placing a dimension and limitation to Light is that we *limit* our consciousness. We can never raise our consciousness to the realization that within the true reality of the Tree of Life and the Lightforce, there is no such thing as time past, present or future. This illusion exists only within the "other body", that of satanic-consciousness.

This time-expansion effect has been confirmed by experiments. Atomic clocks taken on long jet-driven plane flights have been found to log a five billionth of a second behind clocks that remained on earth. While the time lag might seem minute and insignificant, nevertheless, it still proves the point, time is not rigid with its laws. Physicists have already concluded that the closer we get to the speed of light, the slower our watch will run, placing the notion of time in its proper perspective, another illusionary concept of our Satanic-driven rational consciousness.

The problem we face is the lack of a clear statement of the origin of this stubborn concept of time-limitation. The Zohar and Kabbalah have no such problem. The origin of this corrupt and misleading mind rationale comes from no other than Satan himself, the root and arch enemy of mankind.

This idea is so revolutionary that it might well send a shiver down the spine of all mankind. Our conscious mind is under the influence of Satan. This concept may be difficult to accept. However, while we are functioning in the realm of the "Tree of Knowledge of Good and Evil,"[392] we must recognize and deal with the strong role of Satan who deteriorates and debases human values, inflicting chaos and financial ruin, health problems and other breakdowns. He imbues us with the uncertainties in our lives which lead us to the negative activity of stealing, murder and other forms of disorder.

Sure, I know that surrendering our rational consciousness may mean for most of us giving up what we think of as our achievements. However, following on the heels of Zoharic truth, supported by the conclusive evidence of the science establishment, we are never "certain" with our rational mind. Can our rational mind prevent financial disaster or control disease such as cancer and the like? Where can we find in our rational mind a sense of certainty and order in our personal lives? It simply does not exist.

What the Zohar suggests, and religious and scientific lead-

ers refuse to accept, is the concept of a reality called the Tree of
Life universe with the Lightforce. Why are mankind and scientists
so stubborn in refusing to accept the idea of a parallel universe
when all the evidence points to this reality of non-death, non-ill-
ness and no financial collapse? In the absence of anything else that
could stop a runaway universe strewn with rubble and suffering,
why not *try* a revolutionary idea as proposed by the Zohar?

In a section called the *Ra'ya Mehemna* (Faithful
Shepherd), containing the teachings which Moses taught to
Rabbi Shimon bar Yoḥai, the importance of connecting to the
Tree of Life is made strikingly clear.

> "But they that are wise shall understand," [393] for
> they are from the side of *Binah* (Intelligence),
> which is the Tree of Life.[394] And because of these
> wise people it is written in Scriptures:[395] "And
> they that are wise shall shine as the Zohar
> (Splendor) of the firmament, and they that are
> instrumental and responsible for turning the
> many to spiritual righteousness numbering as the
> stars forever and ever."

> *Only* by virtue of your book, Rabbi Shimon bar
> Yoḥai, which is the *Book of Splendor* (Zohar) will
> Israel (the elevated states of consciousness) taste
> from the Tree of Life, which *is* the *Book of
> Splendor*. Only through the instrument of the
> Zohar shall mankind be brought forth from exile
> with compassion.[396]

The Zohar and the Book of Daniel are inextricably
bound up with each other. The language is of Aramaic origin.
Furthermore, we must always be conscious and aware of the fact

that Kabbalah existed long before the idea of all religions came into existence. The written word came into our physical domain with the appearance of the Kabbalistic work titled *Sefer Yetzirah* (*Book of Formation*) authored by the Patriarch Abraham.

Many legends have grown around the power of Daniel within all subsequent religions. One such tradition supported among Kabbalists relates that Daniel and Mordekhai returned from Jerusalem to Persia with the teachings of Kabbalah. They subsequently became known as the written word of the Zohar by the later Sage, Rabbi Shimon bar Yohai.

The Kabbalistic doctrine encoded in the Book of Esther provided the Jews of Persia with the permanent nonviolent weaponry, the Lightforce, by which they overcame the satanic, holocaustic decree of Haman (the coded name for the encapsulated Dark Lord, Satan). The coded Book of Daniel is replete with references to the Age of Aquarius. The Zohar unravels its mysteries.

The secrets that once brought a temporary Age of Aquarius to Persia are now ours. In the present day, we await a permanent Age of Aquarius. Towards the arrival of that date, the Zohar holds out more hope than science that must rely largely on randomness and probability.

The science of the Kabbalah answers many of the enigmatic aspects of nature, yet it remains elegantly simple. The Kabbalistic vision of reality that we have described is based on an in-depth perception of the Bible's coded narrations and tales. The description provided by the Bible sounds quite similar to the description of modern space systems.

This description emphasizes the outer space connection[397] with the Lightforce referred to as the Tree of Life. All the

Biblical incidents suggest concepts that will take us from our familiar world of human experience, the satanic motivator of our rational consciousness of limited logic, to a more subtle, beautiful view of reality that will control the decaying factors within the Tree of Knowledge reality, including eternal immortality.

Rabbi Elazar said: The Lord will one day re-establish the world and strengthen the spirit of the sons of men so that they prolong their days *forever*. As it is written: "For as the days of a tree, so shall be the days of my people."[398]

This is an allusion to Moses through whom the Law was given and who bestowed life on men from the Tree of Life. "And in truth had Israel not sinned with the Golden Calf,[399] they would have been proof against death, since the Tree of Life had been brought down to them."[400]

We can compare this process of undiminished imparting to the kindling of 1,000 unlit candles by one flame. The flame does not diminish in its action of imparting. The wax yes, but not the flame.

The division which is ultimately experienced is a result of and dependent upon the vessels which place their individual stamp of limitation on the energy source. Within the Lightforce or any source of power and energy, however, there is no change. The electric bulb serves as an excellent example of the consciousness that dominates within the corporeal, material realm of existence. The consciousness of either "sharing" or "receiving" plays the dominant role towards the degree of revelation by the Lightforce.

Electrical current normally provides power for a wide range of appliances which may differ in their subsequent manifestation of that power, from a generator to a 5-watt bulb. The question that must be raised is, if electrical current provides sufficient power to drive a generator, then when this same current fuels a 5-watt bulb, why doesn't the bulb blow due to an overload?

The answer lies in the dialogue between the electric current and the bulb. Electric current symbolizes and channels the Lightforce. Any receptacle or appliance contains a consciousness of a desire to receive. Consequently, when electric current is fed to the bulb or any other vessel, a dialogue between the consciousness of the Lightforce, in this case the electric current, and the consciousness of the receptacle, which is its desire to receive, begins prior to its manifestations. The Lightforce is told by the receptacle the amount or degree it is prepared to accept. At that moment, the Lightforce — due to the Kabbalistic doctrine of "no coercion in spirituality" — limits and restricts its degree and intensity to conform to the desire and wish of the receptacle.

By increasing and shoring up the ability of vessel consciousness to push back the Lightforce (restriction), the intensity of the Lightforce becomes vastly increased. The greater the Light's revealment, the greater the pressure on us to reveal it. According to Kabbalistic wisdom, the physical world is just a blip on the endless screen of reality, a temporary static description, a minor disturbance of the Endless peace contained within. The physical reality that mankind experiences is merely a pattern of interference which exists only for a flash of an instant where we live as physical entities.

This is precisely the interrelationship that exists between our physical surroundings and Light consciousness. This interference is the power of the Desire to Receive for Oneself Alone which becomes visible as the material or body consciousness. The universe and man in it are but an enormous composite and picture of thought and consciousness. The universe exists in our minds.

Scientist Sir James Jeans summed it up when he wrote, "The universe was looking more like a big thought than a big machine."[401] Thus, the Kabbalist concludes that the consciousness of the physical body and all matter serves to interfere with our own thought processes, brought on by the consciousness of the Lightforce. At times we become overwhelmed by its (body) consciousness, often completely obscuring the Lightforce consciousness of order, contentment and fulfillment.

When the Kabbalist addresses our physical reality (consciousness of the Desire to Receive for Oneself Alone), he considers the physicality itself to be the universe's handicap, interfering with our daily life. Our entire environment of physical pain and disorder is dismissed as a distortion and in essence it is not even to be considered. It is the consciousness of the "material" force which creates havoc within our universe.

Our conscious attention is generally engaged by the physical objects and thoughts pertaining to the activity of the moment. In addition, unseen influences are having an effect on our thoughts and behavior without the benefit of our Lightforce connection. Kabbalistic teachings offer an opportunity for the individual to become increasingly aware of the danger of unseen influences and, more importantly, to connect with the Lightforce.

These negative, unseen influences, are real and are very much a part of our human landscape. They penetrate the barriers placed within the universe for our protection, whether we refer to these security shields as our immune systems, ozone layers, or other devices established by the Lightforce to balance our universe. These shields can be penetrated or pierced by the Dark Lord and his Death Star Fleet fueled by man's negative energy consciousness, the Desire to Receive for Oneself Alone.

At the precise moment when this interference takes place, the Lightforce must reduce, or remove its consciousness, according to the dictum of "no coercion in spirituality." Free will provides mankind with the possibility of choice between the realm of reality known as the Tree of Life universe or the Tree of Knowledge existence. Once the decision to connect with the Lightforce is made, then the Dark Lord no longer has the energy or consciousness to continue bombarding mankind with his devilish attack of chaos and disorder, illness and uncertainty.

However, once we fall into the illusion of the Tree of Knowledge reality of existence, we are faced with the possibility of becoming vulnerable to their onslaught of devastation. We must be aware, just about every moment of the day, that the moment we permit our thought consciousness to deviate from the Lightforce, we have permitted an opening for the Dark Lord to penetrate our thought consciousness. When that occurs, we begin to actualize the many and varied states of illness and uncertainty in our lives. Our thoughts give credence to the illusion of pain and sickness, financial distress and breakdown.

We must remember that thought energy intelligence is the *only* reality within our existence and mundane lives. We must also understand how the mind, thought-energy-intelligence, can assist in enhancing the welfare of the universe in general and mankind in particular. The Zohar[402] places a great deal of emphasis on the power of thought, to the extent that the major influence towards any recovery from illness depends directly on the state of our thought consciousness. We have the power to maintain financial stability as well as the power to heal.

Due to the quantum effect of the Lightforce, man no

longer is isolated from matters of concern that take place in any other part of the globe. Kabbalistic teachings demonstrate how people can exercise total control over physical realities that were formerly considered not to be subject to thought conscious control. This is the only hope for mankind, to recognize that the future rests entirely on our personal decisions to opt for the Lightforce.[403]

The Lightforce makes no mistakes. The Lightforce does not contain any form of uncertainty or instability. As long as our personal universe attaches to the Tree of Life reality, and we are prepared to accept the idea that we and our personal consciousness can never guarantee our well being, we have taken a great step forward in rejuvenating ourselves and our environment.

If we continue to be snared by the traps the Dark Lord lays before our very eyes, then for the moment that we lie within its trap, to that extent we have lost our ties with the Lightforce. The illusionary tactics of the Dark Lord are a necessary requirement and opportunity to remove and overcome negative energy-intelligence and end permanently the need for Bread of Shame.[404]

Our individual ego is the strongest weapon within the arsenal of the Dark Lord. The reason for this lies in the fact that so long as the Dark Lord can draw our attention away from the Lightforce to concentrate on the self, — *I* do, *I* perform, *I* accomplish, *I* am successful, *I* know, *I* control — then he succeeds in severing our connection to the true quality control of quantum, the Lightforce. Only an idiot can believe his individual ego has absolute control over every aspect that can affect his life and environment, near or far.

And yet, practically all of mankind falls into the illusionary egocentricity of control. The illusionary chaos inflicted upon us by the Dark Lord, sometimes forces us to recognize its effects. A person suffering from the pain and pangs of cancer can find it very difficult to dismiss the pain as illusionary. Easier said than done.

However, what appears more baffling is the illusionary notion of control which the Dark Lord inflicts upon us. How do we reconcile our ego with the visual experiences all around us? How many of us can, by thought, command illness to take a holiday? Financial difficulties or instability have left their imprint strewn along the economic highway of permanent financial success. With all of the obvious monuments both in graveyards and financial magazines staring at us day in and day out, we must ask ourselves where this control is that our egos maintain is ours just for the asking and inserting into our thought-computer.

This leads us to understand the powerful influence the Dark Lord holds over mankind. Despite the overwhelming evidence to the contrary, we still succumb to the illusion that we are in control. If this has been the trademark of mankind since time immemorial, what hope lies ahead for any change in mankind's attitude? Nothing less than an information revolution can alter man's perspective of his thought-consciousness. The Zohar states:[405]

> Alas for the world when Rabbi Shimon shall depart and the fountains of wisdom shall be closed, and men shall seek wisdom and there shall be none to impart it. And the Torah will be interpreted erroneously because there will be none who is acquainted with wisdom.

> Said Rabbi Yehudah: The Lord will one day reveal the hidden mysteries of the Bible, namely, at the

time of the Messiah, "the earth shall be full of the knowledge of the Lord like the water covers the sea."[406]

In this Age of Aquarius, the Zohar holds out more hope than science which must rely largely on randomness and proba-bility. The Zohar, Book of Splendor, provides a direct link and contact with the universal energy-intelligence that we discussed previously. What lies in store for us is an overload of Aquarian energy-intelligence, more intense than any other we have experi-enced.

The reading or scanning of the Zohar will create the adjustable, letter-right personal receptacle that provides us with the ability to receive this awesome power of the Lightforce with-out being burned out in the process. Our failure to meet the demands of the accumulated tensions of daily living, brought about by the crises of modern life, lies in our inability to *secure* the Lightforce within our consciousness. We must develop the full capability of harnessing the Lightforce in order to achieve and sustain fulfillment of life in the midst of these trying times.

Before closing this chapter on the Lightforce let us refer to another section of the Zohar and its interpretation of the Biblical reference to the Lightforce. When referring to the Lightforce, we assumed that, by connecting with the Lightforce mankind was permitted to achieve total control over the universe by virtue of the quantum effect of the Lightforce. Where is this relationship to the quantum effect mentioned in the Bible?

"And the Lord said, Let there be light and there was light."[407] This is the original light which the Lord created. This is the light of the eye. It is the light which the Lord showed to Adam, and through which he was able to see from one end of the world to the other. It was the same light which the Lord showed to King David, who upon seeing it burst forth into praise, saying, "Oh, how abundant is the goodness which thou hast laid up for them that fear thee."[408]

It is also the same light through which the Lord showed Moses the entire Land of Israel from Gilead to Dan.

When the Lord foresaw that three sinful generations would arise, namely the generation of Enoch, the generation of the Flood, and the generation of the Tower of Babel, He put it away so that they should not enjoy it, and gave it to Moses for the first three months after he was born when his mother hid him. When he was brought before Pharaoh the Lord withdrew it from him, and only restored it to him when he stood upon the mountain of Sinai to receive the Torah. From that time on he had the use of it for the rest of his life, so that the Israelites could not approach him till he put a veil over his face.[409]

Anything to which the term *Vayehi* ("and there was") is applied is found in both the physical and metaphysical worlds.

> Rabbi Isaac said: The radiance which the Lord produced at the time of the Creation illumined the world from one end to the other. But it was withdrawn, in order that the sinners of the world might not enjoy it. And it is treasured up for the righteous, i.e., for the Tzadik, as it is written, "Light is sown for the Tzadik."[410]

> Then the worlds will be firmly established and all will form a single whole, but until the time when the future world shall emerge, this light is hidden and stored up.[411]

Thus, the salvation of the world lies in our ability to unite with the quantum effect of the Lightforce. The opportunity has come in our day. The Zohar[412] declares the paradoxical circumstances that will surround mankind during the Age of Aquarius. "Woe unto those who shall be present in that age" refers to those incapable of containing the enormous flow of Light, whereas spiritually-oriented people will reap the benefit of the dawning of this New Age.

The Zohar assigns the beneficial portion of its declaration "praiseworthy are those who shall be present in that age" to those people who have taken control over their mind-consciousness by surrendering to the Lightforce. By restricting their consciousness to the fact that this known consciousness does not exercise or accomplish any control over the environment, and hence, serves no purpose other than as an interference to achieving total control by virtue of uniting with the Lightforce, the paradoxical nature of our universe sets in. By surrendering conscious control, we achieve quantum control. By refusing to let go of our egocentric idea that we are indeed in control, the opposite effect is produced, uncertainty and no absolute control.

> Rabbi Shimon said: The expression "the Lord saw the Light that it was good"[413] means really, "that the Lord decided that the Light should be only good," that is, that it should never be an instrument of wrath.[414]

Kabbalah teaches us the way to remove ourselves from the spiritually impoverishing cycle of negativity, struggle, failure and ultimate defeat. It leads us to a state of mind in which we are connected with the infinite continuum, the Lightforce.

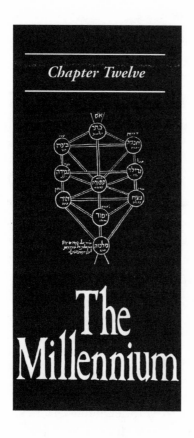

Chapter Twelve

The Millennium

THE APPROACHING MILLENNIUM IS A COSMIC EVENT THAT crosses the calendar every one thousand years. Numerous systems have been devised to keep track of the passage of years. One of the oldest in continuous use is the Biblical reckoning of time. The Bible starts the reckoning of time with the end of the seventh day of creation. The time prior to that could have covered a period of trillions of years. These are not included in the Biblical calendar. Thus, the first millennium occurred approximately 5,755 years ago according to the Biblical calendar.

Each millennium is freighted with enormous as well as profound historical symbolism. The millennium is basically a cosmic event where a one thousand-year epoch yields to another. A great cosmic moment. A millennial year has occurred five times when counting is based on the idea of original Biblical Creation.

The Kabbalah assigns a *Sfirah* (a specific dimension of the Lightforce) to each of the millennial years. The sixth millennium is the *Sfirah Yesod*.

Therefore, there is an undeniable consciousness that permeates and reverberates around the globe with each passing and coming millennium. Time is mysterious and elastic, although it is the organizing principle of conscious human effort. We organ-ize our lives by the clock and appointment books. Yet, little do we realize that time, while elastic, nevertheless is our chance to see, or to imagine, that we see history's narrative framework. Delineated time is the way to make sense out of beginnings, in between, and the finale.

The Christian millennium year of 2000 is almost upon us. While this millennial date is an arbitrary mark on the calendar, people have already begun to wonder what the new frontier beyond 2000 will be; what the future will look like after that moment. Millennial expectations and predictions already appear all around the globe.

According to Biblical reckoning, the year 2000 will begin during the Hebrew calendar year of 5760. On the surface, the year 5760 doesn't impress us with having any deep significance, certainly nothing close to the excitement already being expressed about the 2000 year millennium. Already, party lovers around the globe are booking rooms, making reservations and devising plans for the mega-night.

Where science and technology once offered a future of the fulfillment of dreams, today the future is seen as problematic. The approaching millennium brings with it an increasingly skeptical attitude toward science and a renewed attraction to spiritual values as opposed to material gratification and human excesses.

In recent years the slowly escalating threats of a nuclear nightmare, the vanishing ozone, overpopulation, world hunger and plagues such as AIDS have appeared as this millennium comes to a close. Perhaps our thought and consciousness require a threat of doom to shake us loose from the doldrums that have brought us to this dangerous moment in history.

Whether these catastrophic implications will indeed bring humankind to a rude awakening still remains to be seen. For whatever reason, man has the inclination to jump into the fire rather than flee from it. This has been the steady and continuous landscape that we have created for ourselves. It, therefore, is refreshing to refer to an incredible section among the numerous writings of the famed and sainted Kabbalist, Rabbi Avraham Azulai,[415] and realize that despite our headlong desire to rush into a disastrous situation, this scenario may actually come to a pleasant ending.

Furthermore, the prediction that, shortly, we shall merit the opportunity to reverse the aging process, restore limbs and experience similar miraculous events is no longer in the category of "pie in the sky," although a reaction of skepticism may be expected. Murphy's Law, "If anything can go wrong, it will," remains the centerpiece of Jewish consciousness. This is understandable considering the past 2000 years of Jewish history.

I have always questioned Murphy's Law. Why not create a new law that states, "if anything can go right, it will?" Does this notion seem to be so outrageous or absurd? The answer lies in the fact that we are influenced by the laws of the Tree of Knowledge of Good and Evil[416] whose commander in chief is the Dark Lord.

However, when we abandon the Tree of Knowledge reality, we will shift into high gear and connect with the awesome power of the Tree of Life universe where fragmentation, time zones, and chaos do not exist. There are no *openings* within this atmosphere where the Dark Lord can enter; consequently, things cannot go wrong.

When something *seems* to have gone wrong within the Tree of Life reality, this is nothing more than a *test* to see our reaction. Do we really believe in the Lightforce's ability to maintain order in our lives? Or, do we retain our belief in the Lightforce of the Lord only when things go our way, as if we really knew what is good for us.

The chances that a *change* may come over the consciousness of the Jewish people are indeed slim. Therefore, the Jew is always under pressure from without to undergo changes, even if that means "running from place to place." However, due to the cosmic influence of the Aquarian Age, changes in consciousness have already begun. This is further substantiated by Rabbi Abraham Azulai in his volume, *Hesed L'Avraham*.[417]

> There is a transmission in our possession from the Kabbalists that there are four hundred groups of chaotic packets of energy (*Tumah*). And to remove these groups from their internal energy force requires forty *Seah* (a measure of volume for dry objects and for liquids). And each *Seah* contains or holds 144 average-sized eggs. Thus, forty *Seah* comes to 5760 eggs.

> And since a human being is structured or put together from the four elements (water, fire, air and earth), the cleansing of *any* and *all* impurities (illness, plagues, mental disease) is by virtue of the energy-intelligence of *water*. The reason for this is that Spirit, the *force* energizing these impurities, is

what must be removed and not merely the impurity as stated in Scriptures,[418] "And the Spirit of the unclean shall I remove from the earth." And the internal nature of the force behind these unclean groups is never to enter or come in contact with [the force of] water. When the impurity enters or becomes submerged in water, the spirit-energizer is removed from the impurified entity.

And therefore the Sages required that an unclean person completely immerse the entire body since

even if one hair of the head remains above and outside the water, the impurity remains. The reason
for this is that, whatever groups of negative forces
have taken hold of the individual, when these
impure forces flee from the water and they can still
attach themselves to some part of the body, be it
only a strand of hair, then, when the rest of the
body leaves the haven of water refuge, the evil
forces return and dwell in the rest of the body.[419]

And according to the innermost secrets of the
internal nature of water, the uppermost energy-
intelligence *Ḥesed* (Mercy) is the awesome power
in water's effectiveness to remove and purify any
blemish or impurity, as stated in Scriptures,[420]
"*Ḥesed* (Mercy)[421] and Truth shall erase inequity."

And the waters of *Ḥesed* are drawn[422] from the
attribute and *Sfirot* consciousness of *Ḥokhmah*
(Wisdom).[423] The letter *Yud* of the
Tetragrammaton[424] hints at the *Sfirot* consciousness of *Ḥokhmah*. The form of the letter *Yud* is
like the shape and form of an egg.

The three letters that comprise the spelling of the
letter *Yud* (*Yud Vav Dalet*) have a numerical value
of 144. How do we arrive at the sum value of 144?

a) **The six varied combinations of the three letters
that spell out the sound letter of *Yud*.** Numerically,
these six combinations add up to 120.
[The numerical value of *Yud* spelled out is 20 (*Yud*
is 10, *Vav* is 6, *Dalet* is 4). The three letters of *Yud*
spelled out can be stated in six different combina-

tions: YVD, YDV, VYD, VDY, DYV and DVY. Six combinations times 20 equals 120.]

b) **The eighteen letters of the six combinations of the letter** *Yud.* [The number of letters in the six combinations is 18 (6 times 3)].

c) **The six varied combinations.** Together, the letter *Yud* comprises the energy force of the value of 144. [120 plus 18 plus 6 equals 144.]

Thus, the letter *Yud* and the *Seah* both embody the energy-intelligence of the value 144. Consequently, the *Yud,* as the *Seah,* with its measurement, is capable of removing 10 groups of the spirit of *Tumah* (negative packets of energy). And when forty *Seah* of water combine in a unified whole, they remove, from the individual, the entire 400 groups of *Tumah.*

This idea also reveals the secret of the "four hundred men of Esau"[425] by the Zohar.[426] Also, recognize that at *ten* specific areas in the body, there are gates or entrances by which the *ten* general groups of *Tumah* infiltrate the body and cause the disintegration of the internal and external well-being of the individual.

1) The first gate is at the head.
2) Jaw or cheek on the right side.
3) Jaw or cheek on the left side. These three gateways also symbolize the three upper *Sfirot* of *Keter* (Crown), *Ḥokhmah* (Wisdom), and *Binah* (Intelligence).[427]

4) The right arm pit.

5) The left arm pit.

6) The region where there is hair on the throat
   and on the heart, hinting at the body or trunk
   of a tree.

7) The right thigh.

8) The left thigh.

9) The area of the sex organ.

10) The buttocks area.

These 10 regions act like a throne to the ten groups of *Tumah* wherein these negative energy packets become manifest when an individual becomes *Tamei* (short-circuited). And know that the required measurement for the *Mikveh* (Ritualarium)[428] is 5760 average-sized eggs.

The secret of this matter is as follows: at the end of the year 5760 according to the calendar marking [Biblical] Creation, the following verse shall become actualized. "And the Spirit (Force) of *Tumah* shall I remove from this earth."[429] In addition, the verse, "I will rid the land from dangerous animals,"[430] referring to the spirit of *Tumah*, as interpreted by the Zohar[431] shall also become actualized.

A further secret concerning this matter is that the resurrection of the dead will take place in three stages at three different intervals. The first will be the resurrection of those who are Israelites, buried in Israel. The second refers to those Israelites outside of Israel. Finally, the third is the resurrection of the seventy nations. These periods will be times of intense and great judgment.

And the Third Resurrection will take place at the
end of the year 5760 according to the Biblical calendar.

The preceding revelation speaks for itself. The idea of resurrection or restoring limbs now only awaits the raising of our consciousness towards this miraculous period. The notion that we shall
retrieve our youth should come as no surprise. Those of us stubborn enough to cling to the present ideas of degeneration and disintegration will unfortunately fall prey to the effects of the harsh
judgment days that lie ahead of us.

The lengthy discourse by Rabbi Azulai centers around the
concept of *Mikveh*, containing the awesome power to remove the
origin and essence of *all* negative groups of energy. While the subject matter of this book does not include this awe-inspiring vehicle
for channeling the highest degree of the Lightforce, nevertheless I
feel it appropriate to mention the mystery surrounding the circumstances that brought on an ecstasy of intensity to the sainted Rabbi
Ashlag.[432]

When Rabbi Ashlag achieved a "complete separation from
corporeality," he literally visualized and saw the cleansing process in
operation. He actually saw the water energy-intelligence of the
Mikveh charge forward towards the spirits of the *Tumah*. Terrified,
these negative forces began to flee in retreat towards the "last bas-
tion of hair" not yet immersed within the water.

And when the entire body, including the hair, became
enveloped and surrounded by the energy-intelligence of the water,
these negative spirits were left with no alternative but to release
their hold on the body. They were forced to let go. They no longer

could rely on this particular body for their energy sustenance. The physical domain, represented by those abnormal or dark spots in and around the body, was completely overrun by the Lightforce of the Lord. The camps and bases in which these negative forces resided were now occupied by the Lightforce fleet of the Lord. They were outnumbered.

The required sum and quantity of the troops necessary to remove the enemy was present within the ritually correct water of the dimension of 5760 average-sized eggs. The Dark Lord had no choice but to summon and command his subordinates to completely withdraw from their previously held positions. They were in full retreat. The forces of the Lord began to re-occupy the former locations of their opponents. At long last they were now positioning for the final "mopping-up operations" of the enemy residue left over. The positions were noted and addressed.

Over a period of time, or as long as it would take, the remaining scars and residual trapping left behind by the enemy would be removed, and existing usable tissue repaired and transformed into healthy bastions for rejuvenation of the body and mind.

A front-line view of the preceding scenario was granted to Rabbi Ashlag. The metaphysical barriers and curtains were removed on stage to provide a premiere seat for this incredible battle set within the human body. With access to such a premiere, it is little wonder that Rabbi Ashlag sensed euphoria.

We too, all of humankind, are about to witness the greatest event ever presented on the stage of history. Rabbi Azulai and his discourse shall capture the imagination of all of those seeking a fuller and richer life. The future of humankind hangs in no small measure on the actualization of his prophecy.

The concept of *Mikveh* gleaned from the dissertation of Rabbi Azulai, considers the matter of death and aging as a mystery we often asked about as children, were denied in youth, and reluctantly came to accept as adults. It is considered unlikely or nearly impossible that any of us could live to be 120 years old. Even with the best care it appears that we must grow infirm and subsequently die. While aging is accepted as an obvious fact of life, the causes that contribute to it are not known.

Biological repair systems abound within our physical machine, the body. We are in a constant process of repair, unconsciously or otherwise — from molecules to tissues, or growing our second set of teeth (elephants grow six sets, and sharks an indefinite number during their lifetime). The most visible example of repair to our bodies is wound-healing by which we repair damage to our skin or nails.

Regular replacement goes on all the time at the molecular level. Our proteins are provided with a continuous turnover at a rate characteristic of each unique protein. All linings of our intestines are replaced every few days while those lining our urinary bladder once every two months or so.

At the unperceived molecular level, our genetic material, DNA, is regularly undergoing a repair of some sorts. There are enzymes that restore and repair damaged bases within the DNA and ignore healthy DNA. Hence, while nature is taking us apart, it nevertheless makes every effort to put us back together again daily.

Since many animals, like lizards, can regenerate severed tails, or starfish their limbs, why doesn't the human body undergo this kind of damage control? What prevents us from having lost teeth replaced, like the shark does? Is there any reason why the joints of arthritic sufferers are not replaced as those of crabs are?

Why, for that matter, are we subject to many facets of heart disease, rather than continuous repair?

The answer surely has something to do with the evolutionary process dictated by the cosmic calendar. Medical researchers no longer attribute the higher life expectancy to advanced medical technology. The rapid rise in aging is directly related to the influence of the Aquarian Age. The suggestion of a biological changeover from a normal degenerative process due to aging, to one of regeneration is exactly what Rabbi Azulai is considering.

Biological repair mechanisms seem to be limited only because aging may be *thought of* as simply unrepairable damage or deterioration. We are consciously or unconsciously *preparing* ourselves for aging and death. Therefore, Rabbi Azulai found it necessary, some four hundred years ago, to reveal specific dates when we can expect resurrection and restoration. Consequently, with this revealed knowledge, we, the people will hasten the fountain of youth and observe medical history change before our very eyes.

In the early part of this century, American life expectancy was 48 years. Only a few decades later it is 81. Scientists believe they are the miracle workers of the 20th century. Splitting the atom, antibiotics, computers, heart transplants still have not prevented the state of crisis that envelops the entire globe. Matters have turned from chaotic to catastrophic, while scientists still gloat over their achievements.

Based on current experiments, a number of scientists, are theorizing that, within a generation or two, mankind's life span could be extended by decades if not by centuries. Why? By altering genes, they believe it may be possible to extend and prolong our life. This notion of a dramatic extension of human life arouses healthy skepticism. After many years of confident forecasts, there is still no cure for cancer.

However, could they possible be right? The question has to be taken seriously, but not for the same reasons. A series of discoveries about genes that extend the life of simple organisms, and genes that cut it short, could raise the hopes for advancing life expectancy. However, from a Kabbalistic perspective, no matter what the outcome of these new aging experiments, the final determiner will be the cosmos.

When the moment comes, the aging process will be reversed. This may come about shortly, as stated by Rabbi Azulai. However long the process may take, one thing remains certain: the days of aging and degeneration are numbered. The time factor depends completely upon our awareness and our consciousness. The consciousness and awareness that the resurrection of limbs and bodies is a natural function are necessary for its fruition. With this ingredient Rabbi Azulai's predictions will happen. All physical manifestations of the body are preceded by a stimulus, voluntary or involuntary, and these stimuli are strongly influenced by our belief system.

Researchers who are now asserting that people can live for many centuries with scientific evidence to prove it, neglect the element of consciousness. Why now and not two centuries earlier? We, and this includes scientists, must forego our ego and raise our awareness. We must all come to the inevitable conclusion that cosmic awareness and consciousness are responsible for any successful research and development. This leads to the question, how do cosmic consciousness and awareness come about? And here is where the knowledge of Kabbalah paves the way towards the ultimate goal of "complete resurrection." The answer, fortunately or unfortunately, lies with the people, with humankind.

Is a plague a curse, or an opportunity to remove the plague? Are epidemics signs of punishment from the Lord, or an event to raise our awareness to eliminate the problem? The sole reason for progress has been the consciousness that the problem must and will be solved. The problem of aging will disappear when mankind concludes that there is no valid reason for it being there in the first place.

From time to time, a true genius emerges. Albert Einstein was such a man, the *perfect* innate consciousness. Einstein, like all true geniuses, was *born* with a capacity for cosmic connection. Unlike spiritual-seeking individuals, he did not have to strive for connection, he already had it. But, two questions must be raised. Did he reveal something that had already existed? Or, did he invent something new?

Have Einstein's fellow scientists, by exploring the structure of the universe and devising new hi-sci-tech tools and devices, radically altered the state of existence? No. A genius, far from being the initiator of new concepts and inventions, as commonly believed, is actually a channel for the cosmic unity.

This intellectual energy, in truth, is not entirely the product of the individual revealing the information, but is rather drawn from the enormous input of the collective activity of the human race and the metaphysical energy-intelligence input within the cosmos. In 1905, Rabbi Yehudah Ashlag, founder of the Research Centre of Kabbalah in Jerusalem, decoded the mystery of Rabbi Isaac Luria's theories on relativity and parallel universes. Not by coincidence, only then did science in general, and Albert Einstein in particular, begin their revelations of the general relativity theory.

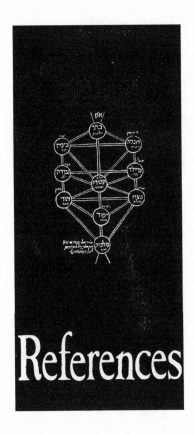

References

148. Zohar I, p.168b.

149. Psalms 102:1.

150. Zohar I, p.168b.

151. Kabbalah for the Layman, Vol.I, Berg, pp.77-90.

152. Kabbalah for the Layman, Vol.II, Berg, pp.161-164.

153. Time Zones, Berg, pp.146-147.

154. To the Power of One, Berg, pp.169-180.

155. Power of Aleph Beth, Berg, pp.180-182.

156. Zohar I, p212b.

157. Genesis 47:29.

158. Zohar I, p.248b.

159. Genesis 49:33.

160. Time Zones, Berg, pp.115-116.

161. Zohar I, p.248b.

162. Power of the Aleph Beth, Vol. II, Berg, p.165.

163. Zohar I, p.248b.
164. Time Zones, Berg, pp.131,132; Zohar III, p.281b.
165. Kabbalah for the Layman, Vol.3, Berg, pp.117-119.
166. Star Connection, Berg, p.49-51.
167. Genesis 23:17.
168. Genesis 2:9.
169. Genesis 4:1.
170. Zohar I, p.54b.
171. Zohar III, p.95a.
172. Astrology: Star Connection, Berg, p.148,152.
173. Zohar III, p.124b.
174. Isaiah 11:9.
175. Zohar III, p.58a.
176. Jeremiah 31:33.
177. Wheels of a Soul, Berg, pp.78-81.
178. To the Power of One, Berg, pp.258-261.
179. Zohar II, p.206a.
180. Power of Aleph Beth, Vol. I, Berg p.110.
181. Exodus 23:16; Leviticus 23:15-22.
182. Zohar I, p.10a.
183. Psalms 34:8-9.
184. Zohar I, p.18a.
185. To the Power of One, Berg, pp.91,92.
186. Isaiah 25:8.
187. Exodus 32.
188. Zohar II, p.81b.
189. Zohar III, p.125a.
190. Gates of Reincarnation, Rabbi Luria, RCK edition, p.52.
191. Genesis 11:1
192. Zohar I, p.25b.
193. Genesis 11:1.
194. Exodus 14:29,30.
195. Gift of the Bible, Ashlag, p.48-50.
196. Zohar II, 7b.

197. Isaiah 63:5.
198. Zachariah 13:9.
199. Zohar III, p.23a, 58a.
200. Exodus 14:10-12.
201. Exodus 14:21.
202. Mekhilta, 14:21.
203. Targum Yerushalmi, Exodus 14:22.
204. Exodus 16:1-3.
205. Numbers 14:23.
206. Zohar 1, p.225a.
207. Exodus 33:20.
208. Zohar II, p.25a.
209. Exodus 6:7.
210. Deuteronomy 4:39.
211. Isaiah 44:6.
212. Zohar II, p.25a,25b.
213. Exodus 14:31.
214. Ibid 16:1.
215. Ibid 16:3.
216. Ibid 16:4.
217. Ibid 16:19.
218. Kabbalah for the Layman II, Berg pp.134-137.
219. Exodus 16:20.
220. Exodus 15:1-19.
221. Ibid 17:1-6.
222. Exodus 14:15-31.
223. Exodus 14:16.
224. Kabbalah for the Layman, Vol.I, Berg, pp.40-43
225. Genesis 3:23.
226. Zohar II, p.50b, 51a.
227. To the Power of One, Berg, pp.128-131.
228. Jonah 2:11
229. Genesis 1:20-23.
230. Kings 2, 2:11.

231. Exodus 10:22.
232. Genesis 1:9.
233. Exodus 14:27.
234. Numbers 16.
235. Genesis 1:14-19.
236. Joshua 10:12.
237. Judges 5:20.
238. Genesis 1:20-22.
239. Kings I, 17:4.
240. Genesis 1:23.
241. Kings I, 17:9.
242. Jonah 2.
243. Leviticus 25:14.
244. Jonah 2:4.
245. Ibid., 1:5.
246. Zohar II, p.198b-199a.
247. Zohar III, pp.200b-201b.
248. Numbers 22:21.
249. Psalms 136:4.
250. Ibid., 98:1.
251. Samuel II, 6.
252. Deuteronomy 31:30.
253. Psalms 98:1
254. Kabbalah Connection, Berg pp.117-119.
255. Talmud Bavli, Tractate Avot,5.
256. Kabbalah for the Layman, Berg, Vol. I pp.76-79.
257. Genesis, 2:9.
258. Numbers 16:32.
259. Ibid 22:28.
260. Genesis 29:2.
261. Zohar III, p.201b.
262. To the Power of One, Berg, pp.85-87.
263. Ten Luminous Emanations, Vol.I, Ashlag, pp.47-51 (1972 edition).

264. Zohar II, p.26a.
265. To the Power of One, Berg, pp.97-101.
266. Numbers 10:35.
267. Exodus 14:25.
268. Deuteronomy, 13:2,3.
269. Exodus 17:8-16.
270. Zohar III, p.152a.
271. Exodus 17:11.
272. Zohar II, p.65b.
273. Time Zones, Berg, pp.168-169.
274. Exodus 17:8-16.
275. Zohar II, p.65b.
276. Exodus 33:11.
277. Exodus 17:12.
278. Zohar III, p.20lb.
279. To the Power of One, Berg, p.4,5.
280. To the Power of One, Berg, pp.210-213.
281. Power of Aleph Beth, Vol.1, Berg, pp.49-50.
282. Zohar III, p.58a,
283. Jeremiah, 31:36.
284. To the Power of One, Berg, pp.169-180.
285. Ibid., pp.2-5.
286. Time Zones, Berg, p.20.
287. Power of the Aleph Beth, Vol.II, Berg, pp.37-39.
288. Astrology: Star Connection, Berg, pp.120, 147.
289. Ten Luminous Emanations, Vol.II, Beginners Tapes, Berg.
290. Time Zones, Berg, p.185.
291. To the Power of One, Berg, p.54.
292. Zohar I, p.36b.
293. Genesis 4:7.
294. Exodus 16:2
295.To the Power of One, pp.181-188 Berg
296. Exodus 15:24.
297. Exodus 16:4

298. To the Power of One, Berg
299. Rabbi Pinhas ben Yair, cf. pp.244-247.
300. Exodus 16:19,20
301. Kabbalah for the Layman, Vol. III, Berg, pp.125,126.
302. Ibid., p.88.
303. Time Zones, Berg, pp.205-208.
304. To the Power of One, Berg, pp. 53-55.
305. The Kabbalah Connection, Berg, pp.25,26.
306. Time Zones, Berg, pp.30-34.
307. Kabbalah for the Layman, Vol. II, pp.154-157.
308. Song of Songs 5:2.
309. Exodus 14:15.
310. Zohar p.48a.
311. Exodus 14:15.
312. Zohar II, p.48a.
313. Zohar III, p58a
314. Jeremiah 31:33.
315. Exodus 14:16.
316. Ibid., 14:21
317. Or Ha'Haim, Kli Yakar, Exodus 14:16-21
318. Exodus 14:15.
319. Numbers 12:3.
320. Nahmanides, Ohr HaHaim Commentaries, Numbers 12:3.
321. Exodus 14:18.
322. Exodus 14:13.
323 .Zohar, III p.152a
324. To the Power of One, Berg.
325. Exodus 2:23.
326. Zohar II,pp.19a-19b.
327. Kabbalah Connection, Berg, pp.133-135
328. Zohar II, p47a,b.
329. Exodus 14:13.
330. Zohar II, p.47a.
331. Isaiah 63:11.

332. Talmud Bavli, Tractate Bava Metzia, p.59b.
333. Joshua 3:16.
334. Genesis 1:19,20.
335. Exodus 14:19-21.
336. Exodus 14:13.
337. Rashi, Exodus, 14:13.
338. Zohar II, p.52a.
339. Zohar III, p.58a.
340. Power of Aleph Beth, Vol.2, Berg, pp.139-141.
341. The Physicist's Conception of Nature, John Wheeler.
342. Zohar III, p.88b.
343. To the Power of One, Berg, p.86.
344. Zohar I, p.13b.
345. To the Power of One,Berg,pp.173-175
346. Power of Aleph Beth,Vol.1,Berg,pp.151-152
347. II Kings 4:18-37.
348. Zohar III, p.91a.
349. Zachariah 14.
350. An Entrance to the Zohar,Ashlag p.32-45
351. Ibid.p.28
352. Ibid., p.29.
353. Ibid. p.19-21
354. Ibid. p.28
355. Kabbalah for the Layman, Vol. II Berg. pp.68-69.
356. An Entrance to the Zohar,Ashlag, p.44
357. To the Power of One, Berg, pp.202-204
358. An Entrance to the Zohar, Ashlag, p.45.
359. Ibid.p.45
360. Encyclopedia Judaica, Vol. 7, p.1383.
361. Zohar III, p.138b.
362. Psalms 147:2,3.
363. Talmud Bavli, Tractate Sanhendrin, p.90b.
364. Kabbalah for the Layman, Vol. I (revised edition), p.88.
365. Ezekiel 27.

366. Zohar I, Prologue, HaSulam, p.48; Talmud Bavli, Tractate Sotah, p.9a.
367. A History of Israel, Howard M. Sacher, Alfred A. Knopf, publisher, 1985, pp.395, 403.
368. Astrology,Star Connection,Berg, p.XVIII
369. Zohar I, p.91b.
370. Psalms 104:31
371. Ecclesiastes 1:9.
372. Zekharya,8:4
373. Zohar I, p.114b.
374. Jeremiah 31:33.
375. Gates of the Holy Spirit, Luria, Kitvei Ari, RCK ed., Vol.12.
376. Kabbalah for the Layman, Berg, Vol.1 pp.4-19.
377. Kabbalah for the Layman Vol.II, Berg, pp.137-139.
378. Lecha Dodi, Friday evening prayer
379. Power of Aleph Beth, vol. 1, Berg,pp.182-185.
380. Genesis 1-3.
381. Kabbalah for the Layman, Vol. I, Berg, pp.53-56.
382. Power of the Aleph Beth vol.2 Berg, pp.29-52
383. Zohar I, p.16b.
384. Ten Luminous Emanations, Vol. I, Rabbi Ashlag, p.124.
385. Ibid.p.58-68
386. Ten Luminous Emanations, Vol.I, Ashlag, p.13.
387. Kabbalah for the Layman Vol.I,Berg,p.8-12
388. Zohar II, p.176a.
389. Malachi 3:6.
390. Ibid.
391. Astrology:Star Connection Berg,p.21
392. Genesis, 2:9
393. Daniel,12:10
394. Power of Aleph Beth Vol.I,Berg,pp.158-160.
395. Daniel,12:3
396. Zohar III,p.124b.
397. Kabbalah Connection,Berg,pp.117-119

398. Isaiah 65:22.

399. Exodus,32:4

400. Zohar I, p.37b.

401. Sir James Jeans,The Mysterious Universe AMS Press Reprint of 1933 Edition

402. Zohar III, p.50a,50b.

403. To the Power of One, Berg, p.74-75

404. Kabbalah for the Layman, Vol. I, Berg, pp.78-80.

405. Zohar III, p.23a.

406. Isaiah 11:9.

407. Genesis 1:3.

408. Psalms 31:20.

409. Exodus 34:30.

410. Psalms 97:11.

411. Zohar I, p.31b,32a.

412. Zohar II, p.7b.

413. Genesis 1:4.

414. Zohar I, p45b.

415. Kabbalah for the Layman, Vol. I, Berg, p.122.

416. Time Zones, Berg, pp./115-119.

417. Hesed l'Avraham, ch. 59.

418. Zekhariah 13:2.

419. Torat Koanim, Parashat Emor, Ch. 4, p.7.

420. Proverbs 16:6.

421. Kabbalah for the Layman, Vol. I, Berg, pp.57,58,63,64.

422. Ibid., pp.57,77.

423. Ibid., p.159.

424. To the Power of One, Berg, pp.20,282,283.

425. Genesis 33:1.

426. Zohar I, p.168a.

427. Kabbalah for the Layman, Vol. I, pp.57,64,76.

428. Ibid., pp.128,129.

429. Zekhariah 13:2.

430. Leviticus 26:6.

431. Zohar III, p.115b.
432. Kabbalah for the Layman, Vol. I, Berg, pg.? see footnote
83.***

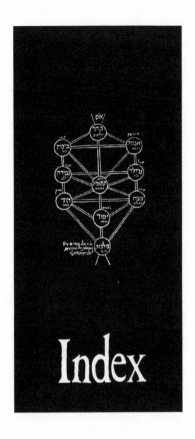

Index